GATHERING GROUND

Lindy —
Enjoy and have ! Let's
a good holidays !
hope fr Peace on Earth !!
XX Patty

GATHERING GROUND

New
Writing
and
Art
by
Northwest
Women
of
Color

Edited by
Jo Cochran,
J.T. Stewart and
Mayumi Tsutakawa

The Seal Press
Seattle

Published by The Seal Press
      312 S. Washington
      Seattle, WA 98104

Library of Congress Catalog Card Number: 84-50806
ISBN: 0-931188-19-9

Grateful acknowledgement is made for permission to use the following previously published material:

"Hsi Shih: Daughter of Silence," by Bee Bee Tan. Originally appeared in *Crab Creek Review*, Vol. 1, No. 1, May 1983. Copyright © 1983 by Bee Bee Tan, reprinted by permission.

"Mirrors," by Nancy Lee Kennel. Originally appeared in *Aurora* magazine, 1981. Copyright © 1981 by Nancy Lee Kennel, reprinted by permission.

"The Image of the Chicana in Teatro," by Yvonne Yarbro-Bejarano. Originally appeared, in somewhat different form, in *Revista Literaria de El Tecolote*, Vol. 2, No.'s 3 and 4, December 1981. Copyright © 1981 by Yvonne Yarbro-Bejarano, reprinted by permission.

"In Order to Survive," by Yvonne Yarbro-Bejarano. First appeared in *Alcatraz 2* (Alcatraz Editions, Santa Cruz, 1982). Copyright © 1982 by Yvonne Yarbro-Bejarano, reprinted by permission.

"The White Horse Cafe," by J.T. Stewart. Originally appeared in *The Arts*, November–December, 1981, Vol. 10, No. 10. Copyright © 1981, by J.T. Stewart, reprinted by permission.

"Partings," by Sharon Hashimoto. Originally appeared in *The Arts*, November–December 1983, Vol. 12, No. 11. Copyright © 1983 by Sharon Hashimoto, reprinted by permission.

"At 102, Romance Comes Once a Year" and "What Goes Around Comes Around" by Colleen McElroy. First published in *Looking for a Country* by Colleen McElroy (Yakima: Blue Begonia Press). Copyright © 1984 by Colleen McElroy, reprinted by permission. "A Question of Vital Statistics" first appeared in *River Styx 15,* reprinted by permission of the author.

Gathering Ground was funded in part by grants from the Washington State Arts Commission, the Seattle Arts Commission, and the Allied Arts Foundation.

Cover artwork by Barbara Thomas, "Three Women Waiting to be Asked to Dance," © 1983 by Barbara Thomas. Used with permission of the artist.

Text design by Rachel da Silva. Cover design by The Seal Press.

Work Shop Printers

Table of Contents

Preface

Dear Reader:

You may wonder what it's like to edit a book like this. You may think that we as editors knew what *Gathering Ground* would look like when we started. As an answer to both questions, we were in a perpetual state of discovery.

As editors we found that we had to come to terms with some frustrating and puzzling realities. What sort of work is representative of women of color? What is special about this work from women of color who are also from the Pacific Northwest? And why is putting the language on the page still so difficult for many of us?

We examined our original guidelines: self-discovery, community perspectives, cultural awareness. We asked ourselves how much should these concepts play a part in the selection of manuscripts. Yes, these guidelines are important, we decided: so much so that we came to see them as imperatives. They are what allow us to define ourselves.

When Jo as an Indian woman spoke of being here in this country the longest that established a context. When Mayumi spoke of the Japanese-American internment, here on the West Coast, in terms of her mother — that established a context. When J.T. spoke of Black people's having been freed from slavery only four generations ago, that clarified our concept of telling time. We were amazed about our own beginnings.

Gathering Ground represents the result of our discoveries — our sense of beginnings, our individual and collective sense of where we are now in the last two decades of the Twentieth Century. We believe that we have become wiser and more articulate as women writers of color. We are grateful that our publishers at The Seal Press (Barbara, Faith and Rachel) have had such faith in us.

Above all, we want to thank all the women who submitted manuscripts, artwork and time. They have helped physically and spiritually to make this collection a celebration for us all — a *Gathering Ground.*

The Editors
Jo Cochran
J.T. Stewart
Mayumi Tsutakawa

Edna Jackson

I have lived most of my life in a small Tlingit town in Alaska. When I was a child, our back yard was the beach and the ocean. If we tired of playing on the beach, my cousins and I would head for the woods and follow the animal trails. My involvement with cedar paper allows me to keep in touch with these two important elements: the water and the woods.

The process of papermaking involves plenty of water, which I thoroughly enjoy, and working with cedar bark, which I break down into pulp for my paper.

Since I am a papermaker with a background in fibers, my very early pregraduate pieces naturally incorporated textile imagery. I experimented with tearing paper into strips and reweaving them, imbedding bits of laces, yarns, and fabric in the pulp to create collages, dyeing pulp for colored paper which I cut up and pieced into traditional quilt designs. I also began to timidly experiment with mask forms that incorporated Northwest Coast art styles.

My early mask pieces were technical exercises; I experimented with different styles of Northwest coast masks, for example, the early Salish style, the Kwakiutl style, the Tlingit style. I feel that these pieces were less successful than my later pieces because they were attempts to duplicate carved wooden masks. It also bothered me that these masks just *sat* on a background and didn't interact with it; they were too static.

At this point, I began to do more with the paper masks' inherent properties. I began to stitch on them, give them ragged and torn edges, distort them while they were still wet, laminate them with flat sheets of paper; they began to have possibilities. I experimented with the length of time I boiled the bark in sodium hydroxide, and used thiourea dioxide bleach to vary the shades of brown I could get in my cedar paper. Finally, I began to incorporate other fiber techniques, such as stitchery, weaving, and wrapping to make my work more personal.

My later pieces use the mask as a focal point, but rather than being the art piece per se, the mask is a single element in a larger structure. They are comparable to traditional Northwest Coast art in the narrative quality.

Working in this manner has greatly expanded the range of possibilities for future pieces. Most appealing to me is the high degree of intimacy and humanness that can be expressed.

Weaver's Mask
(mixed media, fiber construction with hand-made cedar bark paper)

Rainbow/Wings of Different Colors
(mixed media, fiber construction with hand-made cedar bark paper)

Barbara Thomas

Eat the Moon
(pen and ink drawing)

The earliest cave dwellers recorded on walls and carved into rocks the important elements upon which their lives were built: the ritual of the hunt, food gathering, bounty of progeny. In the same voice, I continue the chant, I speak of morning ritual and preparation and its importance to the entire day. I speak of chance encounter and the mad irrational urge to couple with its exclusive pain. Often from a position of comfort, we seek danger and the unexpected . . . we pull it in, and it is the shape of a crocodile. We are at one with joy at the thought of conquering.

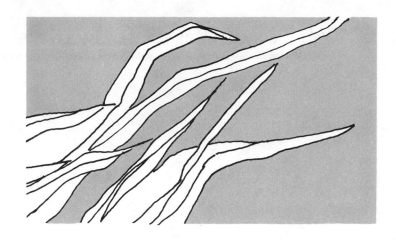

We Cannot Wait
to Be Discovered

"We Cannot Wait to Be Discovered"

Introduction

> "When you make these trips back South," says my
> mother, as I give the smiling waitress my credit card,
> "just what is it exactly that you're looking for?"
> "A wholeness," I reply.
> "You look whole enough to me," she says.
> "No," I answer, "because everything around me is
> split up, deliberately split up. History split up, literature
> split up, and people split up too. It makes people do
> ignorant things."
>
> Alice Walker from the essay "Beyond the Peacock,"
> from *In Search Of Our Mothers' Gardens*

Like most women writers I read a lot and keep notes. I scribble
these quotes in a hardbound notebook and often go back to them
when I find the exact moment that their meaning comes clear in my
work. Sometimes, I use the quote as a preface to a piece as I have
with this one by Alice Walker.

Alice Walker, like many women writers of color who are becoming more widely published and recognized, has played a major
part in influencing and instructing my work. I go to other women
writers of color for sustenance, for a spark and for explanations of
what it is to be a woman of color in American society. Or, most

often, when I need to ground myself again, because the reality of my own vision and life is being lost in the world of academe, job or the white male stereotypes placed on me. So, through reading and through my writing a process has started — a process of self discovery and self defining.

Self discovery and defining of self to me has become a move toward wholeness, toward piecing my life and the lives of other women of color around me together. It means trying to see clearly for ourselves who we are beyond all the stereotypes, racism, and sexism that the dominant white male culture, the feminist movement, and our own peoples impose on us. Then, while grappling with this work, to somehow write about that struggle and the true stories of our self's rising out of it. Instead of wholeness and clarity this process can lead to fragmentation. Because it is hard to be constantly questioning and uncovering yourself, as a woman of color and a writer. So, when I read Alice Walker's words in *In Search Of Our Mothers' Gardens,* my push for a more positive view of my self discovery and definition was defined, and so were my feelings of being fragmented, deliberately.

I began to see how as women writers of color our work can move us to explain and show the danger of these splits in our lives and then to help us fill the gaps that exist in literature, history and consciousness. From my own experience I'm beginning to understand this as a lifelong, continual necessity in my work. Because as long as I, or other women writers of color, cannot uncover who we are, we remain fragmented and not connected to ourselves and other women of color, and all women. Thus we remain separate from our true power. This true power being a strong, growing sense of self, culture and community which can help us take action against racism, sexism, homophobia and other systems of oppression that the white male society has created to keep us in our places.

For some of us the process of self discovery and definition does not have such political or activist-centered goals. Rather it becomes an act of survival, a way to know we exist in writing and in the world, as more than a stereotype, that we stand as individual voices and visions which will help to make up a whole, a chorus that will speak to the Black, Asian, Indian and Chicana women's experience in this country. Writing is a way to know ourselves, to come to be strong in ourselves, and to tell the truths of our realities and visions, and as women of color to fill in our side of the story and world.

Jo Cochran

Bee Bee Tan

Hsi Shih: Daughter of Silence

For Shirley Lim Geok-Lin

> *"In ancient China, it was customary for a court messenger to seek out country women as possible candidates for the Emperor's harem. Hsi Shih was selected from beauties washing by a freezing river."*

In the stillness of nights and wakefulness, we rise
from snoring husbands and quilt-covered children to draw
words into lines. Like night-watchmen who call the hour
we break the silence of generations of sleep-walking
daughters seen but seldom heard and the quiet tears
of maidens snatched from families for imperial harems.

We were silent daughters.
Now we choose paths
by freezing rivers
and walk heavy in men's
clothes with our dreams
and pregnancies on trails
black and narrow as ribbons.
We believe our craft is sharp
with promises for the future.
We hope to germinate and grow
beyond fiction and legends
of beauties of silence.

We cannot wait to be discovered. We will not walk
like Hsi Shih with bowed heads and painted masks for faces.
We are unhampered by full skirts and jewelled phoenixes
and cannot be awed by five clawed dragons etched on silk
or royal pillars to keep the silence of our mothers.

Jo Cochran

Riding Song of One

They speak to you the words of death,
"forget, forget."
Riding alone your ears make voices
out of the wind, *"forget, forget you are."*
This car can't be a horse,
but its night and speed
is what matters, as you knife through the canyon.
You know everything watches this flight,
a tire grazes the rim.
You will not feel it,
"forget, forget you are Indian!"
On the next curve you will break into stars.

This Is Not Simple

for Judith

I hold you with the tenderness
of a Lakota love song. The wood flute
tremors in a fullness of breath.
The music becomes ourselves,
this is not simple, or what we had expected.

So nervous, I'm caught without words.
My thoughts run back and forth as I weave
reasons, magic, hopes
into places I would take you:
La Push mid-August when the moon
brims orange on the water,
Skagit Valley in autumn
and the grey river that can teach
the body to see. I think of quiet
and time for work that calls for doing.
And that we should tell the true stories.
All this wells at the back of my throat.

All this, quickly becomes not you
or I, but a thought-weaving.
I remember my grandmother cautioning me
to be careful, because the things
I wish for might some day be true.

I wished for this embrace,
for it to continue — for our lives
to keep weaving patterns of these meetings.
I wished I could say even the obvious.

Jo Cochran, J. T. Stewart and Mayumi Tsutakawa

Listening In: A Conversation with the Editors of *Gathering Ground*

This conversation grew out of questions we had as women writers of color and as the editors of Gathering Ground. *We couldn't answer all of them, but the experience added focus to our own contribution to the book and became a process we wanted to share.*

M: What makes, what defines a Third World woman writer?

JT: Some definition might limit Third World just to non-industrialized countries, non-white countries. But if I used that definition, I'd had to leave myself out. So here's J. T.'s definition which goes something like this. First of all, the woman has to be a woman of color, which is to say the woman lives in one of the industrialized worlds, east or west, or in one of the emerging nations. I know more about the women who live in the western industrialized world (you know, cutting the universe in half) then more particularly, I'd say about women in this country. And then more particularly than that, about myself. So then I'd have to ask myself, what makes me a Third World writer?

OK, I am one by virtue of that opening definition. And then, I think, too, that I just identify with Third World causes a lot. For example, I went to Mexico with a friend of mine who's also a writer, but she's white. And she has her own kinds of attitudes, but I have to say problems. It wasn't very long before there were a lot of topics we couldn't talk about. For instance, she didn't understand why the Mexicans had so much art in public places and why they commemorated political events the way they did. She couldn't deal with a lot of the murals that were in the palaces and federal buildings that we saw — particularly since the murals were 8,000% political and most of them, if they were dealing with other countries, and in particular with the United States, showed these countries in an awful light.

M: Just ugly.

JT: Yes. They were showing these countries, us, as aggressive imperialists, as colonialists. She could not deal with that, and as a result could not deal with the art itself and then could not deal with political art. I didn't know how to handle it. I'd argue a little bit, but then I'd get real quiet. But I realized how good I felt because I'd never seen art like that which represented, just in huge terms, a visualization of an economic and political struggle. And then because the art itself was huge; I'd seen murals before, but here these were on the ceiling. You'd go up a marble staircase and on the whole wall behind the staircase you'd see something . . . maybe it was Pancho Villa or Emiliano Zapata. And then, too, I noticed the tour guides—that they had a tremendous sense of national pride and so when they talked about their country they were talking about its history and the political things that happened. I couldn't remember, conversely, going through Boston or San Diego and having any sort of perspective on the city in terms of its politics. So there it was for me out in the open. And in the music, too. I can't speak Spanish, I can barely read Spanish, but the poets I like a lot—Lorca, Neruda— are political poets, they are read by the people there. I guess they consider themselves as people's poets. It was an opening-up experience, so different from what I know at home. I'd call that a definite Third World experience for me. It was an enlarging experience— spiritually, aesthetically. I felt a part of the country, too. And I was very glad I wasn't white. But I'm still an American and that's a heavy burden.

M: I have a comment on something that you said but it doesn't really go back to the first question. One of the things that we people of color in this country don't really feel is that sense of national pride. It's very hard for us to feel a part of that kind of thing because even as we are a couple of generations removed from the early immigrants, the earliest people, the tribal nations and so on, we're that much removed that we don't really know what it's like to be a proud member of a nation . . . or to have that pride in an entity or a body. What we feel is some sort of negative feeling towards being a part of a western industrialized nation, exploiting international resources all over the world of the developing countries. So I guess the way to work that into our topic is that we must be feeling some sort of responsibility to Third World women writing—to define this role, as it were: a role which lacks a national pride; a role which defines a responsibility to make our situation known even to the point of hoping that our writing will make our situation better, to make the condition of our people better.

If I must be spending my time to improve my writing, where

must it lead me? It must be leading me to something that I feel must happen. I must use it to improve my people, so I guess even more so as a woman of color, writer . . . having the additional burden of sexism, and so on, just works into that feeling of responsibility.

J: It's been hard for me because I've been getting my act together over the years. And also because I'm mixed blood; I'm Indian and Anglo so I have both sides of the world in my own household; my mother's from a western industrialized nation. But as I get older and think of myself as a Third World woman writer, and knowing that my culture is different, I see the world in different terms. And I think it's because of the responsibility I feel to my people to be able to tell our story—because none of us have had our chance to have our say—to tell the truth with the hope it will bring a unity. I have to create a voice and know that I'm adding in some way to the other writers of color and encouraging someone else. I see how we live our entire lives and how we're different in this country. For me it's like feeling somehow we have a lot in common with the Mexicans . . . because the U.S. came in and colonized us, that they've carried that over to other people of color. I think they perfected that on the Indians and then used it on anybody else who came here. I feel a real strict, loud responsibility to be a writer.

JT: Jumping over on the other side, I think it would be absolutely peculiar if any of my white women writer friends said that they felt a responsibility to their people.

J: They don't know what you're saying if you say it.

JT: They'd say, "What people?" I think also being a Third World woman writer makes you want to search for your own culture, search for what might be called a Third World culture—like one being within the other—and find out what it is. It's out there somewhere.

M: Do we feel a sense of urgency about that?

J: I do.

JT: I only feel it at times which is to say I've got an ambivalence about this whole thing.

(much laughter)

M: Not about being a writer.

JT: (emphatically) NO. Not about being a writer, but I guess about being a Third World writer.

M: (chuckling) Well, you can't be one and not the other.

JT: I know. I know I have no choice. What am I trying to say . . . OK, I always get into the position of having to define myself and I always say I'm a Black woman writer. I understand what being a woman writer means, but for me that doesn't work. Somebody will maybe argue with me and say, "What do you mean, Black writer?" Then sometimes I honestly don't know. It's so much a part of me that I can't explain what I mean. But there're times when it's important, and there're times when it's not. And I'm not sure exactly where that falls.

M: Well, maybe what you're saying is that sometimes in our writing we address very directly the status and history of Third World people, and at other times it's very unconscious or lurking in the background . . . while what we're writing directly is whatever is at hand. But I think it never disappears completely. Now you said you haven't always felt the urgency.

J: The urgency always to be a Third World writer?

M: Or to write about topics that need to be written about?

J: I do, but let's say at times I have a conflict because in order to feel that urgency, I always have to feel politically responsible. I tried for years and years to write a political essay, be it feminist or be it an essay on racism; we've all been asked to write these political essays. But as a poet I don't write a polemic or in a political language; I write in my own. So that's difficult. It's bearing that responsibility for the Third World. So if you're going to be a Third World writer you should write politically or be the next Neruda or Lorca.

M: Yes, I've felt that. It's the expectation of other people.

J: Exactly. Right now I write about my daily life and perhaps that's the point of definition that I'm at. I write about my community life and my tribe around me, and I see that as important. But if I sat down at the typewriter and I said, "Well, today I'm going to continue being a Third World writer," I wouldn't get anything done. Personally, the entire Third World would be on my shoulders. When I sit down at the typewriter, I really have to sit down as myself. And be myself speaking very clearly. Now often, I do want to write a poem about a specific thing that has to do with Third World topics, but it just wouldn't be me. It would just be my bad poem coming out.

JT: I was just thinking about Lorca and Neruda. From what I've read of them, they were political poets but not all the time. And they wrote about a hell of a lot of other stuff, too.

J: People forget that.

JT: I forgot about it, too. They really had a range of topics; they were widely read. Neruda, for instance, could write about pigs, socks (his Elemental Odes), and make a beautiful poem.

J: Look at Alice Walker. She writes about darn near anything. I know a lot of people think of her as being one of the out front, political writers. Or Audre Lorde. I often wonder if women of color writers have a different way of being political in their writing . . . if there's a different way of expression. I've tossed that around in my mind a few times.

M: I think it's important in terms of what we're doing to define the aspects of the Third World woman in this country. A really strong definition is needed. The fact that Third World women are heads of families, there's economic pressure to maintain the family. But at the same time I see women, as through the generations, as carriers of culture . . . an everyday sort of aspect or a long range generational sort of thing with relations, with your mother or grandmother so that you learn these cultural things. I think all of these things are part of the Third World woman that we're talking about.

JT: Are we defining Third World women or Third World women writers? Because I think I'd rather stick with the writers. That's what the whole project's about; that's what we are.

M: That's OK. I'm just thinking that some readers who pick up the book may not even know who Third World women are.

JT: Fine. Good point. In fact, it reminds me of a conference I went to in Ellensburg (Washington). It was a Third World writers' conference and it had been funded by some grant money. It was FREE. All you had to do was pay for the room and board. The room was about a buck a night in the conference dorm they had. And if you could live on chili, you could make it. But they had people there like Frank Chin, Ishmael Reed, Al Young, Lawson Inada, Phil George, and probably about ten others.

The problem was Ellensburg was not ready for Third World writers. (Laughter) The students there at Central Washington University could go and get university credit for the writers' workshops, but they didn't know what Third World meant. So they were totally unprepared for the writers who were there . . . all of whom were quite flamboyant yet sometimes rude or crude because of the accelerating campus/city hostility. The students were just naive to the tee; even the faculty didn't know. In the evening when you had a double barrel reading like Frank Chin and Ishmael Reed, the faculty member would have to stand up and say, "Welcome to the Third World writers' conference." Then there would be a big pause because he or she wouldn't know what to say about what that meant. But as the conference wore on, they began to catch on about what Third World meant, and they were just sorry that the whole thing had even started. It was more than they could handle or want to deal with. And finally there was a big free-for-all at the Thunderbird Motel with some cowboy who wanted to beat up on Phil

George who was dressed up in all his ceremonial (Nez Perce) clothes that night.

J: Typical Ellensburg.

JT: Yes. They vowed they'd never go back to Ellensburg. This was some years ago; in Ellensburg they didn't know what Third World writers meant. I'm pretty sure in a city like Seattle, only a handful of people know what it means.

J: I also think when you're talking about Seattle and the Northwest, we're real different from the rest of the country like in *This Bridge Called My Back.* * Maybe the term Third World women is at the same base level everywhere, but what we think about what we're doing is different here. I think that may be the nature of our region . . . that we aren't as urbanized, as J.T. was saying earlier, that we're not a cultural center in some way. A lot of us are in Seattle or the Northwest for reasons that it's more laid back or jobs are here, or we've been able to make a living for our families. The definition may be the same, but what we're doing is different.

M: You know I don't like apologizing for people of color in the Northwest. When I think of people from the Bay Area or New York I guess they sort of think there's nothing here. I mean that there's no cultural center.

J: I think its focus is different perhaps.

JT: There are cultural centers? Name them. I want to know what they are.

M: Daybreak Star [an Indian center].

J: El Centro de La Raza. And there are some within our own communities. With overt, United States political issues. Maybe it's our age. Maybe we're young as Third World women writing in the Northwest. Maybe the San Francisco trends haven't filtered their way north yet.

M: I don't think there's a way to define how we're different from other places. Sure people here have interests in things that are going on and all over the nation. There are people here who are doing scholarly work or research on ethnic studies that are going on all over the nation.

J: It's not so much that we're different; it's that we're not recognized.

M: Maybe we could take a little different direction here and talk about relations to academia, how Third World women writers

---

* *This Bridge Called My Back: Writings by Radical Women of Color;* Cherríe Moraga, Gloria Anzaldúa, editors, 1981, Persephone Press.

are trained or how they should be trained, or how they're not trained. Jo, you were just talking about the lack of Third World people period in writing programs at the University of Washington.

J: Yes. Right now it's tough to get training at a University, especially the University of Washington because it's so predominantly white male. When you look at the ratio of undergraduate courses, there may be out of 300 chairs in writing workshops for both fiction and poetry—they run three of them each quarter—there may be twenty of them filled by students of color, people of color. When you look at the graduate workshops where I am right now, there are perhaps three—one woman who's coming this quarter, myself and another man. But there isn't anybody to work with . . . well, there hasn't been anybody recently until they asked Colleen McElroy to be a full professor, or conferred that upon her after so many years, which they should have done a long time ago.

Training for us is real difficult because if you go in there wanting to be a writer, they have different skills. If you want to write for yourself and you want to write in your own way which is totally different from what your white male professor wants you to do, usually you come out of workshops writing like the professor. And that's not yourself, so there's this constant battle, I think women experience it, especially women of color—there's this battle to write like yourself yet know that somehow you have to get through school, so you're questioning everything you put down on the page. And you say, is this me talking, or is this the professor?

There's double work going on every time I write something, especially if I write a literature paper. I think that duality, that double work you're charged with cuts a lot of women of color out of the program because you have to start doing that real early as an undergraduate. You can be as radical as you want, up front and outspoken in your writing, but after a time of fighting for yourself you get tired and burned out and you have to quit or you have to look at the things at hand. You have to say I've got children, I've got this at home, I've got to make money, I've got to get out of here, I've got to get back to a job, or I've got to find a job.

Or you put so much energy in it that you become physically ill. I get sick much more when I've in school than when I'm not. It's all the fighting that goes on that wears me down . . . politically and personally. And I'm a lighter skinned person. When I sit in those graduate workshops, they don't know I'm a woman of color, especially if there's a man up there, a white man, so they're cracking racist jokes and I have to be on the basic racist, sexism line of fighting those guys. I basically have to stand up each quarter; I have to whip out my reservation card and say, "Listen, I'm an Indian. Leave me alone, you racist assholes. Go away!" And a lot of women just give up, especially a lot of Indian women who have been in the writing program, who've been anywhere in the University, who've just given up and gone home to the reservation because there's more support there. They end up writing for themselves or small Indian publications. But the university is a system that's a lot like any white system, and the oppression of people of color is built into it. So it's real hard to overcome even though there's a big, big population of people of color at the University of Washington, but you don't see them in writing. They're in business, in communications, I see them in my Women's Studies course, in engineering, in the sciences, but they're never in the arts . . . hardly ever in the arts. It's troubling.

M: I think one of the words you spoke, that's really key is the word support. I think when you're in grad school it's real hard.

J: On the other side of it, the University has been really good for me, but I went in with my eyes open and the word BULLSHIT for about 98% for what they do on my lips. But I've been real forthright and I've been real tough. I think a woman of color going into the University, in a traditional situation, who wants to be a writer has to have armor on all the time, has to be a warrior in some ways because you have to say what you want to learn. And that means you have to be real active in your education. You have to do all the work. You have to seek out instructors. You have to seek out your readings. You have to be real dogged, but that's not a real traditional system. You really have to want some sort of education. For me it's been wonderful; I've been able to study what I want. My first three or four years I was real lost, then I decided I'm tired of this, I'm here paying for this, and I'm paying for it real dearly with all my loans. But it's been good for me because I've had to articulate what it is I'm about.

JT: Wouldn't you say that within that traditional university structure, you've been able to find some non-traditional ways?

J: Oh, sure, I've found the non-traditional ways; I've found the non-traditional people. I went from wanting to teach in English to teaching in Women's Studies, and there're a lot of alternatives there. I've found the handful of professors who will listen and I've found one or two who teach the Third World women writers course. Also if you want to learn prosody, you have the time and the place and the structure to do that. You have someone to say, "This is how this goes" . . . it's hard for me to pick something up just from reading a book. And to have a level of discipline which isn't always in school structures is good for a writer. It's a scale; it kind of balances things.

M: But if you don't take the academic route, what's open? How would a person become a Third World woman writer if one were not in college, and I mean a four year university or college, with or without grad school? Do we have some models?

JT: Do we know women writers like that? Who are these women? Well, Maya Angelou is one of them. If we can only come up with a few, maybe that means. . . .

J: Most of the ones I know have been writers, then gone back to school. A number of Indian women have started writing, then seen that their writing needs more and have gone back to school, but at an older age . . . with their eyes open. They're there for a specific thing so they get in and they get out and kind of know how to protect themselves. Or have support systems around themselves when they go in. Many of the women of color who have a hard time with the system don't go in with some sort of support. Most people say we're crazy when we say we want to write. The alternative would be to do it on your own.

M: I think you can't be a writer completely on your own. You're almost always working in a sort of community group. Let's say you had a community group that wanted to put out its own publication, you're still getting that support and hopefully editing and getting advice within that group setting.

J: Maybe at workshops?

M: Yes, there are some workshops and there are some alternatives to the academic setting, but I think it would be hard to get a disciplined program of studies in which you were expected to produce a certain amount on a certain time schedule without being in school.

JT: Unless it's a school that we don't know anything about.

M: That may be true, too.

JT: For example, let's say it's a professional school . . . I'm coming up with a new kind of model . . . a school that says, "OK, so you want to be a writer?" It's a new kind of A.A. (Associate Arts) Degree.

J: That would be lovely. If there had been one of those around, I would have gone. If there was an alternative university or alternative training system that was taught by women of color or by people of color, or a mixed staff that taught for women writers, I would have gone.

M: Well, hypothetically, here at Seattle Central Community College if there was a program like that, do you think real dedicated people, those with potential, would go into that . . . that they wouldn't need the prestige of a University of Washington M.A.? Do you need that M.A. to get over? Do the publishers want it? Do the people you're writing to grants for want it? Is that not one of the ways we need to get up there on?

J: I think the people you write grants for look for that M.A. I think editors and publishers don't look to see whether you had a university education, if what you send them—the product is good, the words on the page are good—your writing is polished, your voice is coming through. And that you've attained something as a good writer, writing within your own form. They don't care if you have a university degree; I certainly don't as an editor. But there have to be some steps in getting to that point in being a good writer. I think the university can be the most detrimental place writers can be in if they don't know what to expect when they get there. I think the need for a B.A., the M.A., is a hill of beans. I went to the University to study; I just wanted to get a B.A. and get out. I just happened to see that I wanted to study more and needed more time to study. I see it as a way for me to study the things I want to study because the libraries are there. There are courses offered in other disciplines that I'm interested in and I can get into them, let's say in art. I like these courses in that they expand me.

M: But is there community support for some sort of alternative: for example, a workshop that produced a publication, a journal?

JT: I don't know how to answer that. I was thinking when you were talking about somebody who goes to college, gets on the varsity team.

J: Right. Doesn't get an education, but there's all that playing ball.

M: And you have to teach them English. (much laughter)

JT: And then that person becomes a professional sports person. That's the way it's done. It's not done that way in other countries, but that's the route here. So the academic side is just a facade for allowing this sort of activity to happen. Now I don't know if we're using our degrees in the same fashion or not.

M: Hmmn. Are we?

JT: I know those degrees I've got and the places I've got them from have always worked to my advantage; I can't deny that. But I'm thinking underneath that there's something horribly unfair about it. Just because I've got them, they've allowed me to do certain sorts of things.

M: But getting back to the person who decides not to take the academic route, I wonder if they. . . . Well, let's say they're out on a reservation away from any urban center. Do you know some women who've done pretty well?

J: I know women who started their writing when they were living on the reservation but then decided to go to some sort of school to get some polish for their work. Perhaps not that, but to read literature, to find out what the fiction world, the poetry world was all about. They also end up leaving because they find it hard to maintain themselves as women and as writers. As for voice, they find their stories are changing in ways they don't like — that they can't write in their images and in their language. It's hard.

JT: I think the model we've got which is the traditional, academic one is counter productive. I think those of us who have managed to work our way through have simply done that . . . managed. But there's always been a horrible cost we've had to pay for that. I don't want to see that as the only alternative. I'd like to see some other sort of alternative. I think also education is changing. The technology is changing, so that whatever we base our experience on . . . it's simply that; it's a part of history. And to what extent is the education we know going to continue? To what extent should it be the same for all women of color or should it be different for women of color? I think that's something we've got to deal with in this conversation.

M: Well, you've got two really compelling points there. The point about technology is almost self-evident, that everything is moving so fast that we have to be part of it. That's really important. How we get the resources to do that, I do not know; it's not cheap. And as I've heard you say before this conversation, inner-city schools are the last ones to get any computer programs. I went and visited a pre-school the other day where virtually every kid was white and their parents were bringing in the technology to teach pre-schoolers how to use computers. It's the parents; they have their own stuff that they wanted to use. Well, you don't get that in the inner-city.

J: Well, that's something that's been happening for years.

M: You know, it's also white kids having the best equipment — tricycles, roller skates, everything. OK, and that's also something that's self-evident.

M: OK, I'd really like to address some alternatives to academia. Could we propose some kind of positive and forward thinking alternative for what has been a real, for the most part, negative academic experience. And the higher you go in the academic world, the more negative it gets.

JT: And on top of that you have all of those traps to keep women of color out of those schools in the first place. So it's only a hardy few that get in there. And then we have to deal with what happens when one gets in there.

J: We lose our time to write and possibly come in conflict with losing ourselves and who we are . . . our identity. One of the alternatives . . . we've talked about is running a workshop for women who've submitted to the book *Gathering Ground,* and I think on a grassroots level that can happen. I would like for women of color to find some way to get some seed money and start a collective of workshops—like a series. And then from there, networking. As we get the women together in some way and let us see who we are, we'll talk to each other . . . friendships will form. People who live near one another will begin to write and send poems back and forth, or send stories or meet. Smaller groups can meet in between the workshops. Perhaps the thing you'd need is writers who have more experience in one form or another, whether it's academic or not, who are willing to come together and work with younger writers. They can meet with the promise of another conference, and there has to be some sort of way to get funding so that it's made affordable.

We have to provide our own alternative in some way, that the kind of continuing workshop series will be an encouragement to network between ourselves; that it will be an encouragement in the promise that people will read your writing and help you; that the more experienced writers will offer the constructive shaping and criticism that can keep you within your own voice, but can also keep you moving along as a writer.

M: I guess I'm thinking that it should be not formal, but that a person needed to make a commitment of a certain amount of time. Maybe one would have to pay a token amount to feel the commitment. I guess I'm feeling that getting away from academia doesn't mean that you're getting away from discipline. You need to work and you need to show that you have a commitment to it. It's just that we'll take away the biases, the discrimination.

J: Hopefully, yes. I think once you get the women there and you get them writing and you get them interested, and once they see the potential which is there, they'll come. They'll make that commitment because it will be for us in a way that it hasn't been before.

JT: I think there could be some informal kind of thing; maybe participants only came once or twice, but then there'd be other things that would be more structured, more disciplined. I think that's one of the problems women of color have, if they're going to be writers — getting into the discipline of being an artist.

J: We have to learn to take ourselves seriously.

JT: Yes. And maybe in the long run, we are speaking to a pretty large community; it's not just other people in college . . . people taking courses, people going to readings. It's a wide range, from kids to senior adults. In other words, I think we have to have a real sense of audience.

M: For people in the workshop?

JT: Yes and no. As for the larger scope, I think as women of color, as writers, that we have to have some sort of goals or objectives which are different from writers in general. And I think it's a sense of community, a sense of . . .

M: . . . that which we are collectively working towards.

J: I can speak about it personally, but collectively. . . . Collectively we can speak about it in larger terms for a workshop.

(long pause)

JT: Maybe it's like . . . what are some of the characteristics or qualities of women of color writers? We're coming up with a new model here; we're not happy with the old models.

M: You mean, what should the model be?

JT: Yes.

J: What are the potentials, the possibilities?

JT: Yes . . . because in some ways we don't have any choices. For instance, I think being a woman of color writer forces you to be pluralistic; you have to live in a number of worlds. And you have to make those sorts of choices, like move in and out of those worlds with as much ease as possible — which is to say you can draw from those various worlds as you write.

M: Well, for those worlds, I guess we're thinking of the community world, the personal world, the historical world, the academic world, too — the establishment world, so to speak; I think we all touch bases with that world in some way.

JT: For the people who are not of color . . . they don't have access to people of color all that much, whereas we do. We can move in and out of both worlds all the time.

M: We have advantages.

JT: Yes, and so we see things from both sides. And what we choose to write about; we write from that sort of double vision that we have. So we have access, but we're denied access in a lot of ways, too.

M: We're trying to think positively, but sometimes I feel like

I'm skipping around too much. I've got interests here and there; I've got interests in different pies—plus trying to have a family. What can I get out of all this? What should the larger goal be? When does this become a rich diversity rather than a liability?

J: I feel pulled in those directions, too. And there are just lots of days when all I want to do is just sit down. I just want to be a writer (much laughter) and let all of this stuff roll off my back . . . because I have to make a living . . . and so on and so forth. Sometimes it's hard to remember when I did just one thing for a while. That goes back to support; that goes back to having one strong personal center which is hard. It's hard to maintain yourself in that, and it goes back to needing role models to do that. And because I'm a writer in a university, that takes away from having all those strong things.

M: I think the underlying current is that we maintain our craft; that there is a certain amount of work that has to be done; that there's a certain attitude we need to continually improve ourselves. One of the steps towards the future is to maintain that.

JT: And also a place where one can learn the craft.

J: Yes.

M: Do you mean to make contacts, or to learn about the places?

JT: Well, when I talk about learning the craft, I'm talking about just being able to control the language.

J: And the ways you want to control it.

JT: It's just nitty gritty stuff like . . . spelling, grammar, all that, and beyond that into what we call craft. The schools have done an abysmal job with that; yet we're going to need that craft if we're going to express ourselves.

J: Yes, we really need that because when I'm at the University, I take David Waggoner's poetry workshop and he's teaching us music of the language, music of English. He's teaching me an Anglo music basically, Anglo-Saxon music. I hear English, yes, but I also hear Indian English . . . the English I grew up with on the reservation, which is a different music, different intonations from what he's going to have. And so we do need a different place; we need our own centers where we can listen with our own ears both ways.

JT: OK, we can break it down more. We can say that we learn standard English plus the other Englishes that are around. For some of us, it's going to be a totally different language from English. But within these dialects that we call English, there are these other variations, too.

M: I don't think of them as negative things, and I hate being made to feel that things such as the Chinese immigrants' accents are bad. I get a great deal of joy out of hearing accented English, especially around this school (Seattle Central Community College). My son loves the idea that his friends at his school don't speak English; they speak Chinese and they're his best friends.

J: It also makes you feel like you're home for a few minutes.

M: Right . . . one of the positive things I think should be a goal is to work toward publication. That's going to take different forms. I guess I'm wondering what are the possibilities and what kinds of publications we should aim for.

JT: Well, let's say there are print publications on paper; there are oral publications—readings, performances, there are electronic publications. (pause) Maybe that's all.

J: Within the print publications for women of color, you have certain journals that are arriving. You have your smaller community presses, papers—for which you can write articles. These can be creative springboards. You have self-publication perhaps from your own group or workshop. You xerox it, staple it down the side, and hand it out. It gives you a sense of scrutinizing your work. You say, this is the way you want to say it in your own way. Then there are readings which I think are great.

M: Getting back to print. Are there more opportunities within the establishment, let's say in the print media, for people of color to publish in now?

J: Not in the establishment, no. In the women's presses, there aren't any more, but there really aren't any less. It all depends on the funding for a particular year. . . . But in the New York world, now.

JT: But for women of color . . .

J: . . . it's even more no. I don't even think about New York anymore.

JT: What about Seattle?

J: I don't think about Seattle and the establishment world.

M: The economy is just not speaking for you.

JT: So Seattle becomes the microcosm. If we can't find anything here, perhaps that means nowhere else will there be . . .

M: That's what I'm wondering. Is there community support for us, the women of color writers? Can we ask our communities for money? To publish in certain kinds of publications, you need a certain amount of money for a product that will be widely accepted and enjoyed in our communities. Can we look to our communities, or is it a low priority when compared to some of the pressing human needs?

J: I think it's a low priority. In the Indian community, I think you would find money sooner for arts, for woodcarving, for sculpture than you would for writing. Writing within the Indian community, that is creative writing, is not a viable need. Being a good speaker is needed. Being a good grant writer is needed.

M: But I guess I feel the creative writers are needed.

J: I feel they're really needed. But the people who grant you money don't feel that way.

JT: Back to the larger attitude again. The country as a whole doesn't feel it needs writers. If a person is a writer, a person is writing what—romance novels . . . a genre novel; let's put it that way . . . or writing for commercial t.v., something of that sort. That's OK, but for anything else, no. This is not like Mexico or some other country, so we just have a larger attitude to deal with. We have to get around that somehow.

M: So I guess the somehow is to work with small groups of people.

JT: . . . to start changing attitudes.

M: Yes.

JT: We know creative expression is important. Without creative expression you haven't got much of anything.

J: Creative expression holds, maintains, continues your culture—because you're in it, your history's in it, who you are and what you've been, your friends and your neighbors. It's very much in my work. My grandmother's always there, and my people are always there. And to get people within our communities to see that this is what we're doing is a reclamation and a continuation at the same time.

M: That's great. I want to remember that.

JT: I met a former acquaintance of mine on the bus the other day who was telling me about some of the workshop training sessions that he's gone to—that one way you can keep people from achieving is to isolate them. So if you turn it around, if you want a person to accomplish something, you bring the person into the group. The same thing holds true with writing. If creative expression via writing allows you to continue your culture, what better way to alienate you . . . to isolate you . . . than to keep you from doing it. So . . .

J: Think of the power of Black literature!

JT: And in a larger sense, by isolating and alienating writers and creative artists, we as a country kill what there is of American culture.

J: But when you take the other side of it, we all come from cultures in some way—even the large white community—that are based on oral story telling, and we're maintaining our history in that way. In some way that's one correlation that can be made for us — that writers are doing that and that people are strongly united and together when they do have their own literature, our own literature, our own story telling to fall back on. I keep thinking it would be lovely if you could take children and have them in books or in stories told to them, parts of their past — especially Indian children in schools.

There was this Esperanza Estevis who came to talk to my Women's Studies Course about Chicanos and Chicanas here in Seattle. Her seven-year-old son is in the Seattle school system . . . he has Social Studies. At the end of the day they bring in a book, and they were showing pictures which had little paragraphs about Mexico. Her family is newly from Mexico and hasn't been in the States for a very long time. Anyway, her little son kept saying the pictures looked like travel ads because everybody was smiling and happy; the pictures didn't tell you much. How they tend to isolate us is to make the places we come from part of travel brochures. They do it to Indians all the time.

JT: Look at all the Caribbean things.

J: Nothing's realistic. As women and carriers of tradition, that's one of the things I feel we need to do — make our worlds realistic. We need to be telling what's true to ourselves and to our children . . . and getting that published, helping other women do that. You do feel kind of lonely if you're the only one doing it. But America doesn't provide us a whole culture for that we were the melting pot; therefore we didn't need a history which is totally disturbing to me.

(long pause)

M: Anybody have a closing thought?

JT: Can't we just go on?

J: J.T. and I have been known to go on for days.

JT: OK, I think we're talking about transmitting and preserving cultures, but then we're also talking about the vehicle by which we can do that. Now this project (*Gathering Ground*) is very traditional; it's a book. However, there're going to be some new traditions before too long, and I think we want to start thinking about those too. For example, if we take electronic publications, we're talking about video tapes . . . films, both pretty traditional. But we're also talking about computers.

M: You mean for storage?

JT: Yes, but I also mean the way we compose when we write.

The vehicle that we use makes a difference.

J: We can just hook into the computer, and out it comes.

JT: OK, but what I don't want to see happen is people of color becoming more discriminated against, have less access to communication now that technology is increasing. So we have to do something, or else it is going to get worse.

J: Especially if we also want to self publish; all of these things are going to be hooked into the publishing, printing world. And they're going to make it cheaper and easier to do that continually.

JT: Of course I believe other things have to happen, too. Jesse Jackson's running for President is a good example. In other words, there has to be some political context.

J: I think most women of color who are writing see themselves in that way.

M: In what way?

J: After you get past the stage of writing for yourself as as young writer, you begin to see that other things are happening, that your writing is part of Jesse Jackson's running for President — or whatever political movement there is.

JT: Let's go around once more and make some sort of closing comment . . . how we feel as women of color writers.

M: I personally feel a tremendous challenge. To me it's still all ahead. Of course we've all done countless articles, worked on projects . . . but it's all ahead. I don't know what form this challenge will take, but I know I want to keep on improving — either continue more in the journalistic area or to write a play or something different than I'm doing now. I have a family and a small child and I see it in the framework of a ten year period. Perhaps by that time I will have achieved something permanent of a good quality that people in the community will read and find it's not only palatable but valuable in itself. I want it to make a creative statement, yet without deserting any of the values we've discussed this far: knowledge of our history, knowledge of our current condition.

JT: I feel optimistic, too. I feel that I'm looking into the future rather than the past and that whatever I want to do and will do is going to be a revolutionary kind of thing. I don't know what it is exactly, but I know I'm moving toward that. I know I'm paying attention to being a member of the Third World and that endows me with some sort of awesome responsibility, of awesome creativity. It's spooky stuff.

J: I guess for me it's odd that you should say ten years. For me I keep looking forward to the day I'm fifty; I'm twenty-five now. It seems as though fifty has become this place for me. And the things

I'm working with now, I feel I will know something about them. It has been kind of an articulation that comes from the world of a mixed blood . . . a cross-cultural person. My voice is beginning to grow for me and in the Indian community. There are so many mixed bloods in other peoples' of color communities—they have to learn this articulation too. That's one of the things I want to be part of, that articulation . . . also history type projects, history that carries on and traces the lineage of Indian lesbians. It's a building thing, kind of like I'm touching the tips of something and I'm at the very root of whatever it is I'll be doing. And by fifty I'll know. I'm working toward a wholeness that will appear in what I write, and that my pieces will help other people as they will have helped me.

JT: I know that having worked on this book has changed us all, that the result of this process has led to what *Gathering Ground* is, to what we will become.

Kathleen M. Reyes

Queen of Angels

Hospital, Los Angeles

Yolande bears down, and the heat
smells of concrete and cornmeal,
her heat. She will stay.

　　　Aquí, mi tierra –

but blood on the coils
of the low spring bed

　　　mi tierra —

the sirens

　　　mi hogar —

red flecks trailing delicately
on the pinto linoleum
after the blindingly white stretcher bed.

Outside, the heat like the fur
of the slag sky, voracious
bears down. Straps. A bell

of aluminum, fiercely washed
pallid hands, the cupped masks
grinning brightly above her

　　　This one's had her last welfare brat —

Queen of Angels, the stolen madonna
takes to herself a purified novice;

gives her, unknowing, back into the barrio
a little child's gums on her breast
bearing down.

Letter

The letter Kathleen Reyes submitted with her poem "Queen of Angels" summed up so many of the thoughts of women of color and "half white" women discovering their ethnic identities, we thought we would share it as an important part of the voices and directions of women of color in the Northwest.

— Editors

Dear Jo,

I have been deluged with projects here, but I would like to share some thoughts, thinking of *Gathering Ground*. I feel I should describe just where I'm coming from, though. Unlike the women of *This Bridge Called My Back* I am only now coming into a birth of awareness in my identity as a woman of color. The poem I enclose is indicative of this attempt to explore and claim this part of my heritage (I was born at Queen of Angels, but the rest of the poem describes events not *personally* my own.) In this I have been inspired by Ai Ogawa, who has written out of her many heritages even if they are only a small strain of her bloodline: German, Chinese, Black, Choctaw. Also by Sharon Doubiago, who has found a way to write about Southern California. I have always found this very difficult, though I grew up there — lived there, in fact, the bulk of my life up to now. I have lived in the Northwest since January 8, 1979.

My father grew up in East L.A., running with the gangs in the barrios. I still have his high school letter sweater, with "Little Man" embroidered on the pocket: Lincoln Vikings, '51 (he is only 5'2"). He is full-blooded first generation Mexican, and I am his half-blooded daughter of the tidy Mid-City suburbs. He married as WASP as he possibly could, and suffered for many years from terrible nightmares, the devil chasing him for sleeping with a Baptist woman. I am perhaps the "sheltered little wetback" Naomi Littlebear speaks of, but sheltered even from my cultural foremothers and forefathers of Mexico and Los Angeles. (It is also true that I know even less — almost nothing in fact — of my mother's forebears. I have only the knowledge that my only living grandparent is a grandmother.)

I believe that my father saw the only escape from the poverty of the barrio in becoming white, and saw identification with Mexican culture as being destructive and backward to his children. Hence they were taught nothing of this, and saw his relatives with great infrequency — experiences which caused actual culture shock to them. He taught them not a word of Spanish save "Buenos dias Tia Tala" on the single occasion of a visit to a non-English-speaking great aunt.

For many years I have thought this a kind of theft, this erasure of what it means to be half Mexican. Until recently I had thought it a loss, yes, but not one that affected me so profoundly — after all, I am fairly often considered white, aren't I? With all those advantages, right? Why not just go along with it? This was the largest lie, the cruelest illusion of this robbery. In the Northwest, it is true, when people guess my origins they say Jewish, French, Italian. This seems to me a very Northwest sort of erasure; this is a place where most people believe that there is no Mexican-American community at all.

It is the very ethnic homogeneity of Portland which made it the locale where I first considered how profoundly being Latina has affected my very being. At first I noticed only how strange it was to be surrounded by an almost entirely white community, to go for days and weeks seeing only a handful of people of color, and most of those American Indian or Black.

More lately I have begun to realize that though what I have called my "culturally WASP" upbringing did deprive me of language, neither my father nor I escaped our blood. Then, I thought, much of what I knew (and the way I learned to be) was the result of being the daughter of a certain kind of man, but now I see that my wholesale "buying" of patriarchal attitudes, of attitudes I have about myself as a woman — the violence I have known, the accents I have loved, the passion, Catholicism, atheism, isolation, various kinds of stoutness, various kinds of wild loyalty, are inextricably tied up with being Latina and what I did know of this part of my family which includes Mexicano, Chicano, Gypsy, Pachuco.

I have discovered that my wholesale (though unknowing) acceptance that being of color was somehow "bad" has caused me to erase the largeness of this fact in my experience, right down to why some colors or designs appeal to me now, or why I feel mysteriously inadequate in a room full of slim blonde women. I believe that the peoples who went before oneself, who made oneself possible, are ingrained in one's flesh and blood and brain as much as the whorls of the hand or the scar on my lip from being backhanded by my father as a child.

I begin to suspect that my struggles with myself have also been a struggle by the peasants, the *brujas*, the women of Tenochtitlán, the *madres* and *abuelas* of el Pueblo de la Señora de Los Angeles – as they deny having been erased. And, like Cherríe Moraga, I hesitate: "Adrienne asks me if I can write of what has happened with me . . . if I *can*, not *would*. I say, yes, I think so. And now I doubt it."* I also wonder if you will consider this so much the struggle of a woman of color which would fit the aspirations of your book. Being so much Latina does not change that I am part white, and I have a great deal of mystery to resolve in that realm as well. Perhaps you will consider the particular confusion of a halfbreed like myself to be an important area to be addressed by women of color; perhaps you may be interested just now in giving a forum to women for whom their ethnicity is particularly clear, and for whom the things this has meant are common in a particular hard and clear way.

To get beyond the disappearance of other women of color in my life, to no longer fear welcoming them to myself because this would mean accepting a subservient stance toward men (how I hear Cherríe Moraga when she speaks of men being paid attention to "in a particular Latina-woman-to-man way"!*), is tremendously exciting to me. I was slightly alarmed, very honored, and in a queer way relieved to be asked to co-edit the *Calyx* Latina/Native Special issue. It puts me on the verge of something I have long wanted to do. I would like to write more of an essay about the attempted robbery of my Latina self, and how it has been not only trying to get it back, but also the ways it never left me; perhaps also how to speak of being "half" this or that is a deception, the real problem being to reach out to and into all of what one is, and see that one aspect profoundly influences another as the facet of a ruby forks light against and through every other facet. We are too complex to be static insofar as we are alive – to our present selves, our pasts, and our pasts in our ancestors.

As usual, my letter has expanded far beyond the simple desires it expressed in the back of my mind, before I let it see paper. Let me know what you think, anyhow. Take care and good luck with your promising *Gathering Ground*.

Cheers,
Kathleen

---

*Cherríe Moraga, from the Preface to *This Bridge Called My Back: Writings by Radical Women of Color,* edited by Cherríe Moraga and Gloria Anzaldúa, Persephone Press, 1981.

Mirrors

Sun Hyun was already walking when her father decided that she should be weaned. Sun Hyun was already climbing the pear tree when her father decided that she should be married. Without her child, Sun Hyun's mother went into a decline. She peeled the silver off the back of her mirror with her fingers, and ate it. Her hair fell out. Soon after, she was dead.

Sun Hyun's husband was a grown man. Sun Hyun was afraid of him. Their child was born. It was a girl, so her husband named it "Nam Kyung," which means "Felicitous Boy." Sun Hyun's husband spent money at the kisaeng houses on the women and other entertainments. He ran up debts. Without any servants, Sun Hyun cared cared for her baby herself. She cared for her husband. Whenever he spat up blood she collected it in a jar and took it to the doctors.

It was difficult to find suitors for so young a widow. Sun Hyun was blamed for bringing a curse. Her father told her that she should be grateful that he had managed to find her any husband at all. By this time Sun Hyun had stopped growing.

Sun Hyun's new husband became a father for her daughter. Sun Hyun felt what the child felt. When Nam Kyung learned that her new father kept another wife and other children in a nearby town, she hit her doll's head until it broke. After that she did not play with dolls.

Sun Hyun did not worry about the other wife in the other town. Sun Hyun had servants and a real mirror, and a good family name. The other wife had six children, none of them boys, and was losing her hair. Sun Hyun had only one child, but the girl was most beautiful. She had the face that had been her mother's. Sun Hyun worried that her husband looked at Nam Kyung. She asked her husband to send Nam Kyung to school. He visited her there very often. Whenever he was gone Sun Hyun looked in her mirror, and saw her own face growing tired. Bit by bit she peeled off the silver backing.

Nam Kyung's father felt regret. Sun Hyun had been his favorite wife. He changed his plans. He did not bring Nam Kyung home to live when she became of age. He let her finish school. He did not permit himself to touch her, except in the fatherly way.

A man who had been to America was looking for an educated wife. Nam Kyung was older than her mother had been when she died. Despite this disadvantage, the marriage was arranged. Out of deference to his father-in-law, Nam Kyung's bridegroom decided not to get a legal marriage certificate. "We will follow tradition," he said. A wedding was all they had.

Perhaps beause she was older and stronger than her mother had been, Nam Kyung succeeded in having five children. Only one, the oldest, was a girl. Her husband was so pleased that he took his wife with him to America. He had planned to leave her behind with the family.

Nam Kyung was not helpful in America. Her English was not good. At parties she did not make helpful conversation with her husband's superiors. She looked sad when the American women talked about their children.

If Nam Kyung's husband had obeyed tradition he would not have left his wife. If Nam Kyung's husband had obeyed tradition, he would have had two wives. But Nam Kyung's husband called himself an American, and Americans only have one wife apiece. He took his new wife with him when he left America. He did not say what became of Nam Kyung. It would not be polite to ask.

The five children had been brought up in the country by relatives. Only the oldest, the girl of the family, could remember her mother at all. She did not like the American woman her father brought home. The American woman wanted to be liked. She showed the girl all the jars and bottles that she used to keep her skin so pink. She let the girl look at the mirror that she held in her hand.

The girl had never seen a mirror before. All the mirrors in the country house had had the silver peeled off. When the girl looked in the mirror she started to cry. There in the woman's hand she saw her mother's face.

Sharon Hashimoto

Partings

My grandmother speaks my name
slowly, an exotic taste
new on her tongue; asks
again if I have forgotten
anything. I shake my head no,

feeling the heat of the day
bead on my forehead, bake
my skin brown in the silence
that follows. Cool in a sweater,
she watches her hands fold

into a temple on her lap,
remembers in a voice leathery
with sun, of how my father
loved the taste of papaya,
how the juice dripped

from his mouth, made his chin
sticky and sweet. I breathe
the damp smell of Oahu
she sighs into the air. Soon,
I will be gone, pulled away

like the tide from the sand
and she will begin anew
her waiting of long days
swirling into night. She tells
me she will pray until I am safe

in Seattle and I can see her
kneeling, legs bent beneath
the blue print dress, chanting
a sutra as thick as the incense
she will burn. When she rises

her legs will ache until she cups
the muscles between her hands.
Now we embrace, her arms twining
like leis around my neck, fingers
linked in a gentle clasp

and I am afraid to let go
for she will crumble, then I will
forget how for this moment
she is soft as a plumeria blossom,
small as a child.

Flower Arranging

Snow white chrysanthemums bowed low,
spoke to me of you
with scissors in your hand
and frogs in the bottom
of the hand painted vase.
You croaked in your reedy whisper
of tall flowers that mean the heavens;
medium stalks, the earth;
and short blossoms, man.
I stared as your hands
clipped and bent
the world to your will,
wondered if this was how
you shaped me.

I gather daffodils and bluebells,
mingle their voices with baby's breath
and bring them to you,
lying among stones
of marble and granite
that grow closer each year.
There were fresh cut roses
on newly turned earth
when they buried you
like treasure in a sea of green.
Reverend Hamasaki's elegy
floated over waves of grass,
rose and fell in the syllables of a language
I felt but did not understand.

Your bones are in this land:
turned to ash, you nurture
the seeds you planted,
watch them sprout deep roots
and lean towards the sun.
Thoughts of you
hang from blue and white clusters
of wisteria twined above the door
where I ran past pots and trowels
with yellow dandelions in my hand
to your side.
You wiped the dirt
from my cheek, smiled
and said that I was homegrown.

Vickie Sears

Adolescence

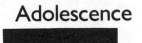

In peddlepusher days
I'd stand in front of the mirror
nipple pinching
pulling them to encourage growth
envied classmates with burgeoning blossoms and
evidence of training bras
barely shadowed beneath their blouses
snapped by boys amid laughed whispers.
oh well
I'd content myself with pubic hairs
all of ten or so
and wondered if anyone knew what was happening to my body.

it took forever to convince mother that
one of stepfather's white sunday churchshirts
worn only at funeral mass or easter
was a necessity to match
rolled-up bluejeans and penny-crested loafers.
dad said I was like a greenbay packer and that was
the best someone who looked like me could hope for.
I'd adjust my glasses with a humph
bury hurt
leave to play baseball
where I was invincible in running
fast as spit splitting the wind.
if there wasn't a game,
I'd run in the hot of the day awhile,
mom wanted me in the sun,
then make my way through the window of
my room
where waited all the secrets of the world.

there were movie magazines about people from the
1920's through the 1950's
pill bottles filled with bugs so I could be a scientist
a backless panda bear where treasures were hidden
prayer books with rosary beads for the time I wanted to be a nun
secrets of my body to explore
despite the threat of wart covered fingers
so I could be a woman
and cosmopolitan and seventeen
which assured me of what I needed to know of
how to catch and love a husband
because just having a man was wicked.
there was paper and pencils
to weave a life where it was
alright to be a girl and not a linebacker.
poems spilled from a midnight pen
scratching by flashlight under the covers.
there I was Dickinson, Brönte or Woolf
good and powerful
true to whoever I was
knowing I was lovely.
I took all the magazine tests on
how you got along with your husband
I always did well.
then came the curse or
riding the white bunny
as my mother euphemistically called it.
it interfered with baseball.
brought sweetsmiles from mom's friends with
chimings about being a young lady and
not letting anyone touch me
lectures from dad which presumed I'd be somehow bad
and his nickname of basketball boobs.
I hated it
I loved it
there was a secret everyone knew
but only I could feel
it promised other worlds to which a cosmopolitan prince
would whisk me.
did it show?
sing the treasure of itself?
powerful gift
bringer of admonitions

secret weapon
for what I never knew.
what an awesome event
that's what ladies home journal called it all
participant in a miracle
I waited to get pregnant
but nothing happened.
oh yes,
the problem was
I didn't have a husband.

Pubescence at 39

Went to dinner with her thursday.
liked what i heard
saw.
sorted out all day friday
wanted to be sure i interpreted her correctly
agonized in case i hadn't.
spent saturday worried about what the rules might be.
how long did i wait?
what shall/should i say?
waited to confirm with my therapist.
then decided to call.
that was wednesday.
a first date phone call
i sweated
my palms bled fluid.
what if she said "no" or worse "yes"?
she did!
now what?
by thursday night i had set up a fire in the fireplace
waiting for a monday match.
friday, at 1:30 in the morning,
i began to clean house
washed the sheets
just in case

put out a towel set
took it down
put it back
three times
finished at 5:30 am
slept on the couch,
to keep the sheets clean
slept there all weekend.
saturday found me buying as wide an assortment of
vegetarian food as i knew
carted it down the stairs
put it away to seem all natural in my meat eating environment
stood back to admire the stock
panicked
how do i cook this?
went to the bookstore for a cookbook
subgums and glutinous
didn't sound good.
put flowers all around
made a tape 120 minutes long.
just in case.
sunday i took the towels down
put them back up and down
three more times.
got the theatre tickets monday.
if i hadn't would she have wanted to be with me anyway?
like a woody allen script
i'm ready for this
first date.

Grandmother

Her house smelled of
    woodfire
    wet dogs
    old medicines.
    "aaay" she'd smile in
    brokentongued english.

"english dumb. stupid english."
it never stopped her stories.
they drew themselves out of her
diminutive four and a half foot frame,
rolling in the lyricism of their own telling.
she sat in her rocker
children before her
candle between her feet,
which threw menacing shadows
up
across her face
arched along the wall
onto
the ceiling
where they danced at momentous moments
as she
rocked for effect.
she told coyote tales of fire theft,
of the great dog spilling stolen food and
making the milky way,
the magic of changers,
of the water beetle's part in creation
and
how two legged people came to be
moving us to ecstasies
our eyes almost in pain with wideness
at her tones,
matching hand stroked etchings of
mountains
water fallings
running creatures
anything Grandmother wanted to show.
she didn't need the english
on which she had such a fragile hold.
it was the drama of her time
that filled our needs.
katydid keeps the tongue cherokee
hears our tales of then and now.
my memory hears Grandmother's
"aaay"
and smiles.

These Women Only Look Crazy

See that sister
with her chest
hanging out
buttocks
exposed to rain
wind and white men.
She used to
dream of dancing
shaking
her lean torso
undulating with
The Dance Theatre of
Harlem.
She used to
dream like the
nappyheaded baglady
sleeping at the
police station
her swollen ankles
thickened by
pantyhose made for
white women.

Once she had
wanted to plant
her funky body
in front of a
microphone
and wail wail wail
sing downhome
Mississippi blues
like Bessie Smith
but in her own
key.
What about that
Black bikini
wearing woman
with a pierced
nose and pressed
hair
who used to
dream
before her
husband-lover-roommate
brought home
a teenager's baby.
She used to dream
of painting
a moist brush
blazing hands
drying hands
across a canvas
spilling color
a portrait of her
own still
life. .

And there's that lady
marching up and down
fifth avenue
with the headscarf
around her neck
heavy coat and nursing
shoes keeping
her safe
on the hostile
streets at night.
She used to
dream
of sculpting a montage
in earth and clay
red dust from Georgia
to brighten
the effect.
She used to
dream of pressing
now gnarled fingertips
into wet
stone.

I am sorry you are
proud of the man
who raped your
great-great-great
grandmother and left
your hair good.
Please, this is not
envy it is sorrow
for the long road
we must travel
to be sisters. My
lineage can be traced
through the roots
of my hair to
Nairobi. Do not
try to make me
ashamed of this
fact, sorry my hair
grows in dry tight
cottonfields on my
head and will not
fly in the wind
like the woman I am not.

Wedlock

Being married is the pits
you say while your tongue
tries to slice at my flesh.
But I bide my own time and
hum "lord how long?" as I
gather my strength like
a good squirrel with nuts.
So each time you throw
stones or toss spikes in
my heart and want me to lick
my own wounds while you come,
I gather my strength like
a good squirrel with nuts.
Oh yeah,
I'll be ready
come

    winter.

Essme Thompson

Black Lesbian Journal – A Passing Scene

Saturday. Elaine had been at the womyn's bar since eleven thirty P.M. Not that it was very crowded, but it had taken one and a half hours before she got a seat at the bar. She sipped her beer and smoked a small cigar. When both were done, she got up to stretch her legs, leaving her jacket to mark her seat taken.

She stood against the wall and stared at a dykey-looking Chinese womon dancing with a possibly gay boy. Not getting much response, she had smiled at the womon before. Maybe they were hetero after all. A womon came by, a familiar looking womon who said as she passed by, "Don't get too excited." Elaine stared after the womon who returned to her seat. 'What did the womon mean by that?' she thought.

She looked at the womon who was now sitting at a table of Black womyn, hers the only white face there. Curiosity aroused, Elaine returned to her barstool. An older white butch sitting next to her started talking. Ignoring Elaine's refusal, she bought Elaine another beer. While the butch kept talking in her right ear, Elaine mentally shrugged and turned her back to the bar, staring out into the crowd at the womon who had spoken to her.

Then she saw the white womon rise and walk over in her direction. The womon was about her height though her blondish afro hairstyle made her seem a bit taller. The womon came straight up to her, held out her hand. Charmed, Elaine took her hand and followed her to the dance floor.

It was a slow love song and the lights were dimmed. They moved close and slow together, and Lionel Ritchie sang about how truly in love he was. After they danced, they came back to Elaine's bar stool and talked. The womon said her name was Leah.

Elaine listened to Leah tell bits about herself and grew bored until Leah said something that hooked her attention. Above the blare of the renewed disco music, Leah said she was a Black womon who looked white and that it provided her with a special set of problems. Elaine was intrigued. She had heard about people like that but hadn't met any as far as she knew. She assumed that most passed as white, having only white lovers. They traded phone numbers, and Leah went back to her table.

Now it was about two and Elaine was still drinking beer at the bar. She felt a touch on her shoulder. Leah was there with a short-haired blond womon beside her. "Do you want to leave with me?" Leah asked. Elaine looked at the other womon who frowned at her, possessive vibes like daggers coming from her eyes. Elaine was puzzled. She was sure Leah had said she was single and lived with a roommate. She hadn't mentioned anything about coming with any-one. "No, I'll call tomorrow," Elaine said. Leah looked at her hungrily and left.

Sunday. Elaine got up early to attend the eleven A.M. planning meeting for the Womyn of Color forum, wishing she could sleep till noon. Eleven was no time to be anywhere when one had hit the bed at four.

Home again at two thirty. She had told Leah that she would call between one and three. Tired and burnt out, she sat and thought about the womon she had met last night. A white-Black lesbian? She wondered if Leah told white womyn she was really Black? Or did she pass. It was possible. Leah had eyes that were light-colored, blondish nappy frizzy hair, lips that were full but certainly not Negroid, a white-looking nose. Was Leah really Black? Or had it been a line to hook her as it had. The whole thing seemed funny, but Elaine wanted to investigate more. She called.

Ten minutes later Leah came. While they were talking, Elaine examined her closely in the daylight. No, Leah didn't look a speck Black. She looked white down to the broken red capillaries on the end of her nose. Leah was stretched out on the couch as Elaine sat in a hard straight-backed chair. She wanted to get the womon out of her apartment gracefully and suggested going out for some coffee to help keep herself awake.

"A deal if you give me a kiss," Leah said.

'Oh, well, what the hell,' Elaine thought and entered Leah's open arms. They tangled on the sofa, kissing and hugging. Elaine told a few bad jokes to defuse the moment. Leah invited her to a potluck dinner that was to happen at six thirty. Again Elaine said "Coffee," and got up to put her nikes on.

There was coffee and talk. Leah suggested pool, so they went to a bar to shoot pool and talk more. Leah ordered her a Spanish coffee with 151 rum. It made Elaine sleepy again. Leah said she had been raped twice, once when she was ten years old. She had been estranged from her mother and bounced from foster home to foster home. She had a violent streak in her. Now she was thirty-five, a Pisces. She worked in construction, asbestos. Leah seemed to want to impress Elaine with her wealth and bragged about making twenty-five dollars an hour. Elaine disliked people who thought money would dazzle her. Working in cable t.v., she had made good money in her day and didn't believe Leah made that much.

Elaine guided the conversation. They talked about religion, life after death, hitch-hiking, Leah running guns for the Black Panthers, a bit of everything which gave Elaine a better idea about her. Leah was trying very hard to please her and say the right things. Elaine didn't know what she could believe about this strange womon who seemed to want her so badly.

They had the potluck dinner at the friend's house. Leah brought a six-pack of beer. At about seven thirty Elaine was tired and wanted to go home. Leah drove her home. She wanted to come up, but Elaine had had enough of her for the night. Already half asleep in the car, Elaine pleaded sleepiness and said, "No."

"How about tomorrow? Do you have anything planned?" Leah begged.

'Holy shit,' Elaine thought. "O.K., but don't call until after noon." Leah looked pained but agreed and kissed her goodbye. Elaine got out of the car.

Monday. Elaine's phone rang at twelve minutes after noon, waking her. Cussing and knowing it was Leah, she let it ring itself out and tried to sleep again. Unable to sleep, she turned on her bedside t.v. wondering what she had gotten herself in for. At twelve thirty the phone rang again. She answered it, growling. It was Leah inviting her out for breakfast. Elaine refused; she wanted part of her day to herself. She suggested eight. Leah agreed reluctantly. At six, Leah called to invite her out to play pool with a couple of her friends. Elaine said she still had to eat dinner. Leah said she'd come by in an hour. Again Elaine agreed reluctantly.

Elaine and Leah shot pool and drank beer for about an hour or so. Leah's friends were an Oriental womon from Hawaii and another womon who looked half Oriental, half Black. When Leah asked Elaine where she wanted to go next, Elaine suggested the womyn's bar where they had first met. Once there, Leah ordered a dinner and a bourbon for herself; Elaine had a bourbon also.

Leah told a tale of some womyn who had once spiked her drink with LSD and then, sending her on a bum trip, freely fucked with her mind. For vengeance she'd gotten a $100 car, invited her friends for a ride and driven the car into a wall. Leah got a cut knee;

her friends got a large hospital bill. Elaine, keeping her face expressionless, simply said, "I see." But inside she was blown away. If the story was a lie, that was bad enough, but she thought it was more the truth. What kind of person would risk her own life to get revenge for a trick? More and more she felt Leah didn't have both oars in the water.

Something else was funny too. Tonight Leah said she lived alone. How come she had 'forgotten' about her roommate, the short blond-haired womon? Nothing was worse than a bad liar who couldn't keep her lies straight. This would be the last time Elaine would keep company with Leah. Also Leah now said that her telling white womyn she was really Black didn't come up, so she never said anything. Here Elaine had been thinking Leah was a sister who identified with her Black sisters, despite her looking white enough to pass. But it just wasn't so. The spark of Elaine's interest was cold and dead.

Now she heard Leah saying she wanted to grab the weed she had at her house and go to Elaine's. That was the last thing Elaine wanted; she knew she couldn't stand to have Leah in her house again. While Leah drove them across the river to her place, she thought up excuses.

Leah lived in an apartment close to the railroad tracks. As she opened the door, she asked Elaine to excuse the mess. A wave of fetid odor greeted them. The kitchen was a disaster area of unwashed dishes and stale food. Hiding her disgust, Elaine smoked a reefer and listened to Leah talk. There was violence under a thin surface in this womon. Leah kept handguns laying around in the living room. She kept a rifle in the back seat of her smelly garbage-filled car. Her kitchen smelled like her car.

Leah kept on talking. When she said she now wanted to go over to her place, Elaine asked why. Then came the confession. Leah did have a roommate and since there was only one bedroom, they slept together. But she swore there was no sex involved. She and Betty, the womon she had been with Saturday night, were just friends. There was no sex involved, she repeated.

Elaine had two rules: don't get involved with womyn living with womyn, and never sleep with anyone crazier than she was. Leah hit it on both counts. She saw a way out of this mess. Very gently she explained that she didn't get involved with womyn who shared a bed at home with another woman. Leah was a nice person, but Elaine's intuition had told her to let this relationship pass. Leah pleaded again that she and Betty were just friends; there was no sex. Elaine shook her head. "I can't go against my intuition. I always get into trouble when I do."

Leah bent over, hiding her face in her hands. Elaine sighed quietly. She was tired and she had a headache from the smoky bars. The clock said almost midnight. Just then Betty came home. Leah lifted her head and greeted her. Betty didn't speak but went into the bedroom. Elaine didn't turn around. "Can't we just make love tonight?" Leah asked.

"That would be getting involved," Elaine answered quickly.

"Well, can we just sleep together and not make love?"

Elaine was worn out by this womon. She was like an open wound, bleeding psychically all over the place and trying to hook Elaine with guilt and sympathy. Elaine didn't like to be manipulated that way. "No. Why sleep together and not make love? It's my rule not to get involved this way in such a situation." This time she was less gentle but still firm. Leah was definitely not the type of womon Elaine wanted, not with all those lies, her craziness and her violence. "Now that I've said no, does this mean you're not going to drive me home?" Elaine said in a joking way.

Leah looked at the floor. "I'll drive you home," she said.

During the ten minute drive, Elaine was silent. Leah talked about how all of her friends knew she and Betty didn't have sex. Elaine could ask them. They would tell her. Elaine thought about not caring to take a sexual survey of Leah's friends. She just wanted to be alone. Finally at her apartment, she said goodbye to Leah who just looked at her with a face of stone and a crazy glint in her eyes. Elaine remembered the rifle in the back seat. She kissed Leah's unmoving lips and said goodbye again. Leah didn't speak or respond to the kiss. Elaine got out of the car. She didn't turn her back on it until Leah had driven away.

Homecoming

Father, I came home last night.
But the dog was not at the gate.
The servants were gone. I waited.
The rain rattled on banana leaves,
and palm trees leaning on the wind
soughed like the sea.

You were very late,
and I could not stay.

Later, I listened to that empty house
breathing the dark.

Sunday Morning, Banilad

You said your body hurt,
a stranger
imposing on you.

We cast our lines
where circles broke the pond,
and waited.

I answered,
things change.

The mountain stretched her body
in the sun,
nursing young clouds
at her breast.

You hoped
for better.

Birds burst
and dove
into a golden field.

Of course, I said.

Far, the surf was gentle –
or was it the wind?

We sat and waited.

Fish ran circles
around the sun.

Lisa Furamoto

In Grandma's Bedroom

In grandma's bedroom, time stands as motionless
as the constant smell of incense
which lingers in the still air.
I am always eight years old
as I walk through the doorway.
I can hide behind the soft pile of futons
in her closet and the moth balls
will still make me sneeze;
I can climb on the sturdy iron frame
of her firm double bed then brace
myself between rail and ceiling
and pretend to be a tightrope walker
in the big three ring circus;
or I can sit on the bed's edge
and gaze up at grandpa's picture
in its heavy oval wooden frame
and wonder why they say
I remind them of him.

The floor creaks as I walk towards the candlelight
of the hotokesama, the household shrine,
where the first servings of this morning's rice,
pressed neatly into domes in small brass cups,
are offered to grandpa and his two sons.
Japanese scriptures from Honpa Hongwanji
are displayed in front of the Buddha.
A string of wooden beads with a tassel, the geizu,
lies next to a brass pot of ashes
in which sticks of seinko stand,
the curling ash of their burning white tips
sending threads of smoke streaming upward.
I place the geizu around my hand
then tap the edge of the brass bell
delivering a soft tone which slowly fades
as I sprinkle incense shavings
over the seinko then place my palms
together and whisper a prayer three times.
Specks of burnt candlewick drop
into the melted wax and circulate
leaving delicate trails of grey.

Amy Nikaitani

As I state my philosophy on my art I feel it is important to state my philosophy toward life, as both are intertwined.

As I approach the last third of my life, I am contemplating life and the quality of my life. I look towards retirement in the near future and I feel a deep need to change my way of life. I need to leave behind all the hustle and bustle of the middle third of my life, a time of raising five kids and going to work, with my art sandwiched in between. (My art has provided me much needed quiet time; it is my meditation, my tranquilizer, my equalizer.)

Looking at my life, I see that I have been brainwashed to think that we should hustle and bustle to achieve status, hustle and bustle to have fun, run ourselves into the grave, and then when we die, go to heaven and we will have time to lay back, know peace and tranquility; God will take over and it will be wonderful. This is no longer what I believe I will find. I feel this is just something made up to make life seem more endurable through hard times.

The life hereafter is now, peace and tranquility can only be now. Coming to the last third of my life, I am so thankful that this realization has come to me. I cannot take credit for this awareness—I gratefully acknowledge what my daughter, a retired kindergarten teacher named Olive Jorgens, and a man called J. Krishnamurti have contributed. I have watched my daughter, a graduate school dropout, struggling to shed the programming that I as a mother and others in her life have imparted, to uncover a more meaningful way of life. This meaningful way is the natural gift of life, given also to me, but from which I have so deviated.

And so, as I enter the last third of my life, naively and optimistically, I may continue growing in my art, or I may find it was only a temporary refuge in my search for a peace I need to find. In my present state, my feeling is that I will never lose my love of drawing the human figure, nor give up my search for beauty through my work.

Claire's Break Dance
(ink sumi drawing)

Amy Nikaitani   69

Ondo I
(mixed media drawing)

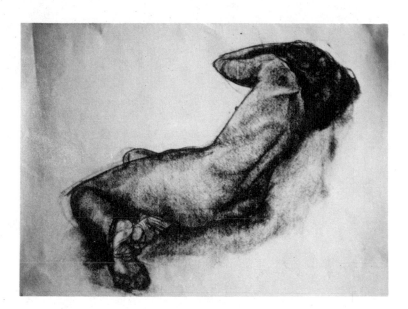

Nude
(charcoal drawing)

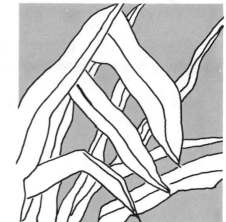

I Am Going to Talk With Them About Their Daughters

"I Am Going to Talk With Them About Their Daughters"

Introduction

As a minority student activist at the University of Washington in the early 1970s, I joined others in challenging established practices with our youthful zeal and budding political theories. But as middle-class Asian female university students, we sought the insight, perspective and direction we could learn from "the community." Since we lived away from the community and lacked experience in facing the harsh reality of discrimination in housing, employment and a myriad of other ways, we students referred to "the community" as both our source of street wisdom and our raison d'etre.

We fought our battles in the name of "community." But what *is* community?

First, the community may be defined as the pockets or settlements of ethnic minority groups in the United States. Or, secondly, by the fact that most of these people's skin color differs from the majority's (in America) shade of white — thus the term "people of color."

But looking beyond the overly developed shores of America, one discovers the "developing" countries — Third World countries — from which immigrants, slaves or contract laborers came and whose descendents form the community of Third World people in the United States: a third way of looking at community.

In discovering and expressing community, women of color writers in the United States must remove the blinders forced upon us by traditional education to see the similarities we share with other writers of color due to the history of racism. We must learn that we are part of the Third World.

In discovering community, we focus our sights on a worldwide picture, in which we find that people of color are indeed the majority. We also come to realize that people of color over the past few thousand years have created outstanding achievements in technology, art, philosophy and political theory — only to have these achievements obliterated by a few recent centuries of the white man's greedy, systematic and ruthless destruction of the Third World.

On a smaller scale, we discover community in Seattle, in Portland, on the reservations of Eastern Washington, in the fishing villages of Alaska. We women of color writers find that we cannot deny the persistence of community — encompassing this local history, these achievements, this struggle against racism — which runs through our work.

In reality, Third World women face many important responsibilities in life besides sitting down and writing about the past, present, or future "community." The nurturing of families, ensuring economic survival of these families, in addition to the role of perpetuating cultural and spiritual aspects of our peoples, often falls squarely on the shoulders of the women of the community. Thus, studying and writing has been subservient to the survival of our peoples.

In earlier times, the women's stories of the community were passed to the next generation by way of oral history and songs, weaving, drawings depicting village life, letters to relatives or personal diaries. Many of the stories and words of these early women of color writers are just now being discovered, partly because of the low status such items have held within community structures.

The question arises: What community support do women of color writers now receive for their labors? Sadly, the answer must be, not enough. Lack of time, lack of money, lack of appreciation for the artistic, along with undisguised sexism, create tall barriers that keep women of color writers in the Northwest and elsewhere from achieving their goals and dreams as writers.

There are other barriers as well. Although many community women may have the desire to express themselves, to stretch their imaginations, to put forth intellectual questions through poetry, fiction, essays, plays, or criticism, few have the opportunities to learn, to train, to develop their skills. Few have the connections or the access to grants and publications, to teaching positions, to role models who could help them develop into first-rate writers.

At the same time, technological advances in communications — such as electronic word processors, new photographic equipment, videotape cameras and recorders, sophisticated typesetting equipment — are only beginning to make inroads into our communities. The majority white society still controls the complex tools of this fast-paced industrialized world, and our communities will be unable to keep abreast without setting a priority on developing funds and expertise for these tools.

We need to encourage and build these means of discovering, studying, expressing, and recording the history and creative aspects of our communities. We need to work with women of color writers to help them gain control over the skills and tools needed to become accomplished writers. This book, *Gathering Ground*, is a start. A community school for women writers might be another focus, with readings, classes, mutual criticism sessions and guest teachers to provide inspiration and insight. This would lead to a new generation of women of color writers, creating and expressing our community stories. Certainly, our communities deserve no less. Certainly, their impact would go far in combating the false and demeaning images white American society has set aside for women of color.

Mayumi Tsutakawa

Bee Bee Tan

One Woman Waits for Spring Blooms

In the last month of the monsoon,
we hide from the downpour
in a small dark room in Kuala Lumpur.
Our fingers clutching sepir skin,
we cling to each other, and listen
to trains rumbling in and out of the station.

We eat our pickled love knots
of deep-fried twisted pork intestines.
The motion of the train sickens me
and I am sure it is our child within me.

Up north, I left you at the railway
station telling you, "it is no easy
thing to be a woman."

I drink the juice of moongrass
brewed in an earthen pot for a waking day.
I taste bile on my tongue;
my mouth is colored yellow,
but where is the flow I yearned for?
Three times, I double the dose
but the pulse grows stronger.

In my sleep, the fetus wraps itself
around my neck like a snakelike strand of rattan.
Its unformed face puts its lips to my mouth.
It is like a fish covered with virgin slime.
Everywhere I look, I see flaming flowers
òf the forests, red as menstrual flows.
In the morning, I see my belly
expanding beyond my clothes.

Sand reflects the glint of glass and light.
I rock in my chair,
mangrove trees shading the front porch.
My belly extends beyond the tips
of my rattan armrests.
I have finally learned to rock a gentle motion,
waves from the nipah fan in my hand
as I wait alone for new spring blooms.

One Woman Talks About Her Children

One woman, hair colored by peroxides,
dressed in Thai silk,
sits at a teak table,
pouring tea out of a sterling pot.
She waves her carefully painted nails
matching the thin stretch of her lips.
Adds exactly one teaspoon
of extra fine granulated sugar to her tea,
and speaks of her children.

Irene, a real beauty,
just graduated with an accounting diploma
from Tar College in Kuala Lumpur,
still makes the best lotus flower soup
and won't date anyone without a car.

A diamond grape cluster at her throat,
this woman leans toward the subject
of Fred her son, the engineer.
The light picks up glints of grey in her hair.
She remembers him chasing butterflies,
and now skirts,
not unusual for boys
who should have their fun.
But daughters, she whispers knowingly,
should never be allowed abroad.

Patchouli, The Scent of Moths

From the light of evening, the woman slides
into the bar shutting out the smells of Seattle's
waterfront. She flutters in like a moth or copper
butterfly in a riot of colors and the sweat
of night already clinging to her hair, a mass
of frizz, reeking of Patchouli. This woman is full
of excesses and does not attend to subtlety.
She lounges at a table, her fingers soothing a drink
and I can almost see in this amber light,
the prostitutes who lounged at street corners in my town,
squeezed mint leaves into pouches the way this woman must
squeeze her hips into jeans. The musk of her perfume
floods the room as if its smell could hide
her faults and I remember how my mother brought me moon
pads scented with three drops of Patchouli just enough
to cloak the smell when I looped the ends into my belt.

In the afterchill of brandy the woman rubs her arms
and her scent rises, I see grandmother who coated
her arms, rubbing in pungent oil to kill the larvae
of brown-tailed moths. In the outhouse, grandmother
polished the seat with burnt Patchouli. Idly, the woman
whose tan has faded swings her necklace, its beads
red as the cinnabar moth whose colors do not warn
of its taste. Now she wraps the light around her
and her perfume weaves its tendrils towards grinning men,
longshoremen with clean cuts and professors filled
with their own importance. They do not see the sores
behind her ears or smell her breath thick and sour
as lime twists trapped in Gin Slings.
They are captivated by this woman, gaudy as rafflesia
flowers and baptized in the noisy smell of heavy musk.

Her orange hair sparkles in the heat of the bar like eyes
painted on the wings of Malaysian vampire moths that breed
in swamp heat. I drink cappucino and its fragrance
is lost in the heavy mist of her Patchouli,
so like the medicine grandmother lathered on my bruises.
Beyond the French windows, Puget Sound mirrors fish factories
with smells that match this woman's scent, foul as the parasitic
rafflesia, whose tropic petals beckon wide as a man's arms.
As children, we learned from our grandmothers to tread
carefully around gaudy flowers whose beauty distracted
us from rough leaves. We learned to grind stems for Patchouli
oil and always we followed moths and butterflies who drew
us by their scents to deadly flowers growing large
and leafless with the fluted scales of night.

Blue Dream
(pen and ink drawing)

Evelyn C. White

Frances E. W. Harper:
Black Feminist Pioneer

"If Sojourner Truth was a blind giant, Frances Harper was an enlightened one."[1]

The experiences and achievements of black women represent a very important segment of American history. Yet few Americans, black or white, male or female, know anything more than the most rudimentary facts about the most famous figures. For instance, most have *heard* of Sojourner Truth, Harriet Tubman and Mary McLeod Bethune. It is not likely, however, they know that Harriet Tubman fought in the Civil War and is the only woman to have ever successfully carried out military strategy behind enemy lines; that Sojourner Truth was born "Isabella" in upstate New York to slave parents who told her stories in low Dutch, their only language; that Mary McLeod Bethune, pioneer educator, built her famed college on a garbage dump with a $5 down payment.

Ours is, unfortunately, a culture that has not placed much value on learning, understanding or analyzing society through its historical traditions, individuals or events. It is not surprising then, that those of the lowest rank, black women, have suffered the most comprehensive and devastating historical neglect.

It is a well-worn, but well-heeded saying that history repeats itself — especially regarding the history of oppressed minorities. One need only consider Martin Luther King, Jr. — an oratory rebel cast from the molds of Frederick Douglass and Paul Robeson; Watts — as fiery as Nat Turner's 1831 rebellion; Angela Davis — a freedom fighter in the tradition of "Moses" Tubman; Nina Simone — goddamning Mississippi in the same manner Bessie Smith sang her "Washerwoman's Blues"; or "unbought and unbossed" Shirley Chisholm — a political power surely from the inspired lineage of nineteenth-century poet, reformer and lecturer Frances Ellen Watkins Harper.

"I know of no other woman, white or colored anywhere,
who has come so intimately in contact with the colored
people in the South as Mrs. Harper. . . . In the colleges,
schools, churches and the cabins not excepted, she has
found a vast field and open doors to teach and speak. . . .
But the kind of meetings she took greatest interest in
were meetings called exclusively for women . . . indeed
she felt their needs were far more pressing than any
other class."[2]

So limited is our historical perspective that it seems odd to say
that Harper was born to *free* parents on September 24, 1825, in
Baltimore, Maryland. Unlike her contemporary, Sojourner Truth,
Harper had no first-hand knowledge of slavery. Her awakening, her
impassioned battle against the "peculiar institution," sprang from a
symbiotic response to the suffering of all members of the black
race. As a black woman, Harper knew she did not have to be a slave
to *be* a slave, and she fought to rectify that injustice all her life.

Orphaned at age three, Harper was raised by a minister uncle
who indoctrinated her with the ideals of Christianity, work and
freedom. Her book *Moses: A Story of the Nile* (1869) and much of
her other poetry reflect religious themes. At thirteen, Harper left
her uncle's home to work, as was customary for free black girls.
She made her living as a nursemaid and continued to educate herself as best she could. Harper was twenty-five years old in 1850, the
year that Congress, after much heated debate, passed a law provid-
ing that: 1) California should enter the Union as a free state; 2) the
other territories would be organized without mention of slavery; 3)
Texas should cede certain lands to New Mexico; 4) SLAVE-
HOLDERS WOULD BE PROTECTED BY A STRINGENT FU-
GITIVE SLAVE LAW; and 5) there should be no slave trade in the
District of Columbia."[3]

This law, officially the Compromise of 1850, but referred to
almost exclusively as the Fugitive Slave Law because slavery was
indeed its most volatile issue, had an extraordinary impact on
Frances Harper's life. She later said:

"Maryland had enacted a law forbidding free people of
color from the North to come into the state on pain of
being imprisoned and sold into slavery. A free man who
had unwittingly violated this infamous statute had recently been sold into Georgia and had escaped thence by
secreting himself behind the wheel house of a boat
bound northward; but before he reached distant haven

he was discovered and remanded to slavery. It was re-
ported that he died soon after the effects of exposure
and suffering. . . . Upon that grave I pledge myself to
the anti-slavery cause."[5]

Simply put, the law required all American citizens to return run-
away slaves. A slave who had braved the brutality, bloodhounds
and bounty hunters of Georgia to arrive in the "promised land,"
could be seized and enslaved again. Such was the zeal of some
slaveholders because of this law, that it was not uncommon for
them to attempt to enslave blacks who were born free or had lived
free for years.

The passage of the Fugitive Slave Law of 1850 demonstrated in
no uncertain terms that freedom was an arbitrary condition; that
blacks would never be free until slavery was abolished, if then. The
slavery controversy predominated the decade leading up the the
Civil War. Stowe's *Uncle Tom's Cabin* (1852), with its depictions of
the cruelty of slave owners and privations of slaves, won thousands
over to the abolitionist cause. Black abolitionists like Frances
Harper joined with white abolitionists to oppose slavery, eventually
forming their own Anti-Slavery societies. Though William Lloyd
Garrison and Harriet Beecher Stowe found slavery abominable, it
was obviously free blacks who suffered much more from the subju-
gation of their race.

"A hundred thousand new-born babes are annually
added to the victims of slavery; twenty thousand lives
are annually sacrificed on the plantations of the South.
Such a sight should send a horror through the nerves of
civilization and impel the heart of humanity to lofty
deeds. So it might, if men had not found out a fearful al-
chemy by which this blood can be transformed into gold.
Instead of listening to the cry of agony they listen to the
ring of dollars and stoop down to pick up the coin."[5]

Harper began to lecture for the Maine Anti-Slavery Society in
1856. By then she was already widely known because of her poetry.
Her *Poems on Miscellaneous Subjects* had been published in 1854
and she frequently combined her speeches with recitations from her
poems.

"The sale began — young girls were there
Defenseless in their wretchedness,
Whose stifled sobs or deep despair
Revealed their anguish and distress.

And mothers stood with streaming eyes,
And saw their dearest children sold,
Unheeded rose their bitter cries,
While tyrants bartered them for gold. . . ."

In the poem, "Slave Auction," from *Poems on Miscellaneous Subjects,* Harper makes her point with more personal poignancy than she does in her speeches. But both were strong in their emotional appeal, forcing the reader or listener to see that black children were being stripped from their mothers to maintain the Southern economy.

From 1854 to 1859, Harper lectured extensively throughout the Eastern seaboard. William Lloyd Garrison's Boston weekly, *The Liberator,* recorded information about her speeches. In 1860 she married Ohio farmer Fenton Harper, gave birth to a daughter, and was widowed four years later. With decreased domestic responsibilities, Harper "like a warrior continued to fight the great enemy of her country — slavery."[6]

The Civil War began with the bombardment of Fort Sumter in April 1861 and ended when General Lee surrendered the Confederate Army in 1865. The entire social, political and economic fabric of American life changed during the war and the Reconstruction period that followed. Over four million slaves had been emancipated. Though Lincoln had hoped to colonize a substantial number in Africa or South America after the war, no serious plans for such a transaction had ever been developed. Moreover, most blacks had no desire to leave the United States. Many had fought in the Civil War for their liberation and intended to work the land, educate themselves, attain the ballot and participate fully in American life.

Frances Harper was in great demand as a speaker after the Civil War. She traveled throughout the South and saw, as she had not previously, the particular plight of black women. Unlike Sojourner Truth, who had drawn parallels between the abolition of slavery and women's suffrage early in her career, it was not until Harper had her "Southern awakening" that she became specifically concerned with the role of black women.

> "This part of the country reminds me of heathen ground, and though my work may not be recognized as it was in the North, yet never perhaps, were my services more needed; and according to their intelligence and means, perhaps never better appreciated than here among these lowly people. . . . I am going to talk with

them about their daughters and about things connected with the welfare of the race. Now is the time for our women to begin to try to lift up their heads and plant the roots of progress under the hearthstone." [7]

In the Reconstruction South, black women continued to bear the brunt of the labor burden as they had during slavery. "Colored Women in America," an article by Harper, was published in the *Englishwoman's Review* during this period. Her impressions were as follows:

Mothers are the levers which move in education. . . . They labor in many ways to support the family, while the children attend school. I know of girls who iron til midnight that they may come to school in the day. Some of our scholars, aged nineteen, living thirty miles off, rented land, ploughed, planted and then sold their cotton, in order to come to us. . . . In the field women receive the same wages as the men, and are often preferred, clearing land, hoeing or picking cotton with equal ability. When work fails the men, the money which the wife can obtain by washing, ironing and other services, often keeps pauperism at bay. I do not suppose, considering the state of her industrial lore and her limited advantages, that there is among the poorer classes a more helpful woman than the colored woman as labourer.

The inequitable division of labor was a concern at the first women's rights convention held in Seneca Falls, New York, in 1848. The women's rights movement was, however, overshadowed by the slavery controversy and did not resurface until after the Civil War when privileged white women and newly freed black men found themselves in competition for the right to vote.

Frederick Douglass had given a major address at the first convention and was greatly admired by Susan B. Anthony and her suffragist friends. However, during Reconstruction, when there was increased hostility and resentment toward blacks, Anthony found it politically expedient to disassociate her movement from the enfranchisement of blacks.

"In our conventions . . . he [Douglass] was the honored guest who sat on our platform and spoke at our gatherings. But when the Suffrage Association went to Atlanta, Georgia, knowing the feeling of the South with regard to Negro participation on equality with whites, I myself asked Mr. Douglass not to come. I did not want to subject him to humiliation, *and I did not want anything to get in the way of bringing southern white women into our suffrage association.*"[8] (emphasis mine)

Though Anthony's sentiments were guised in the rhetoric of "protectionism," it was simply racism, a racism that predominated the suffragist movement from its inception.

When Sojourner Truth spoke at the second women's rights convention in Ohio in 1851, it was in opposition to many white women who felt that the former slave, representing "the two most hated elements in society" (black and female), would hurt their cause. "Again and again, timorous and trembling ones came to me and said, with earnestness, 'Don't let her (Sojourner) speak . . . it will ruin us. Every newspaper in the land will have our cause mixed up with abolition and niggers, and we shall be utterly denounced.' "[9] Truth's legendary "Ain't I A Woman" speech was partly in response to members of the audience who ridiculed her and attempted to laugh her off the speaker's platform.

Harper, educated and refined compared to Sojourner Truth, commanded a bit more "respect" from the white suffragists. Nonetheless, it was clear to her that they would never fully support the emancipation of blacks if it jeopardized white women attaining the right to vote. "Mrs. Harper said that when she was at Boston there were sixty women who left work because one colored woman went to gain livelihood in their midst. . . . If the nation could only handle one question, in view of the peculiar circumstances of the negro's position, she felt his rights might fairly be considered to have precedence."[10] And remarkable though it may seem, such was the case. Blacks were granted suffrage by the 15th Amendment in 1870: "The right of citizens of the United States to vote shall be denied or abridged . . . on account of race, color or previous conditions of servitude." The word "sex" was not included. It was not until 1920, when the 19th Amendment was ratified, that women were finally given the right to vote. Frances Harper "discovered" racism in the suffragist movement, as she had discovered the status of black women when she began to lecture in the South.

In 1871 Harper settled in Philadelphia, where she continued to campaign for women's rights and the temperance movement, and to write:

And if any man should ask me
If I would sell my vote,
I'd tell him I was not the one
To change and turn my coat . . .

But when John Thomas Reder brought
His wife some flour and meat
And told her he had sold his vote,
For something good to eat,

You ought to see Aunt Kitty raise,
And heard her blaze away;
She gave the meat and flour a toss,
And said they should not stay . . .

You'd laughed to seen Lucinda Grange
Upon her husband's track
Whe he sold his vote for rations
She made him take 'em back.

Day after day did Milly Green
Just follow after Joe
And told him if he voted wrong
To take his rags and go.

I think that Curnel Johnson said
His side had won the day,
Had not we women radicals
Just got right in the way. . . .

This poem, "The Deliverance," is from Harper's *Sketches of Southern Life,* of which four known editions appeared between 1872 and 1896. Her novel *Iola Leroy or Shadows Uplifted* was published in 1892 and was, until the very recent discovery of Harriet Wilson's *Our Nig* (1859), the first novel to be published by an Afro-American woman.

Iola Leroy is the story of an octoroon (the offspring of a quadroon and a white) girl who was raised as white, but then enslaved when her father died.

> "I never had the faintest suspicion that there was any
> wrongfulness in slavery, and I never dreamed of the
> dreadful fate which broke over our devoted heads. . . . I
> found that my father was dead; that his nearest kinsman
> had taken possession of our property; that my mother's
> marriage had been declared illegal, because of an im-

perceptible infusion of negro blood in her veins; and that she and her children had been remanded to slavery. I was torn from my mother, sold as a slave, and subjected to cruel indignities. . . . I am constantly rousing myself up to suffer and be strong. I intend, when this conflict is over, to cast my lot with the freed people as a helper, teacher and friend. I have passed through a fiery ordeal, but this suffering will not be in vain. I am a wonder to myself." [11]

Like Harper, the protagonist Iola Leroy was unconcerned about slavery until she was confronted by it in a personal way. Leroy reflects her author's activism in that she pledges to help her people and commits herself to reformist work. Compared to Wilson's *Our Nig,* however, *Iola Leroy* is a fairly sentimental work. Whereas the Leroys resign themselves to their tragedy and look to a better life in God's heaven, Nig directly attacks racism and divides white society into absolute categories of evil and good.

"From early dawn until after all were retired, was Nig toiling, overworked, disheartened, longing for relief. She wore no shoes until after frost, and snow even, appeared. . . . Any word of complaint was severely repulsed or cruelly punished. It was Mrs. B's favorite exercise to enter, vociferate orders, give a few sudden blows to quicken Nig's pace, then return to the sitting room with *such* a satisfied expression, congratulating herself upon her thorough house-keeping qualities." [12]

Our Nig; or, Sketches from the Life of a Free Black, In a Two-Story White House, North, Showing that Slavery's Shadows Fall Even There, is a rebellious, angry work. Its full title clearly reflects the author's bitter sense of irony. *Iola Leroy* has a passive, much more conciliatory tone and as such is in keeping with the attitudes and experiences in Frances Harper's life.

In the early years of Reconstruction, Harper wrote to Thomas Hamilton, editor of the *Anglo-African:* "We have the brain power, we have the muscle power, and in all rebel states we have political power. If our talents are to be recognized we must write less of issues that are particular and more of feelings that are general. We are blessed with hearts and brains that compress more than ourselves in our present plight. . . ." Though the phrase was not born until almost one hundred years later, Frances Harper had defined the essential elements of black power. Throughout her long career as an activist and writer, she crusaded as fervently for black people as any figure from the more recent civil rights era. In her later years, Harper's black activism found expression in her participation with the Women's Christian Temperance Union and in her leadership in the National Association of Colored Women. She was a supporter of Philadelphia's Frederick Douglass Hospital and promoted the Colored Authors and Educators Association and other similar societies that sprung up at the end of the nineteenth century.

In Philadelphia, there is a house at 1006 Bainbridge Street. On December 8, 1976, it was named a National Historical Landmark. It was the home of Frances E. W. Harper. Sixty-five years after her death, we realized a black woman was deserving of that honor.

Footnotes

1. Monroe A Majors, *Noted Negro Women: Their Triumphs and Activities* (Chicago: Donohue and Heneberry, 1893), cited by Janey Weinhold Montgomery in "A Comparative Analysis of the Rhetoric of Two Negro Women Orators — Sojourner Truth and Frances W. Watkins Harper" (Fort Hays Studies, Kansas State College, December 1968)
2. William Still, introduction to Harper, Frances E.W. *Iola Leroy or Shadows Uplifted* (Maryland: McGrath Publishing Company, second edition 1969). Original published 1892. pp. 1–2
3. John Hope Franklin, *From Slavery to Freedom: A History of Negro Americans* (New York: Alfred A. Knopf, 1980) p. 200
4. Frances E.W. Harper, cited by Montgomery, Op. cit., p. 41
5. Frances E.W. Harper, cited by Montgomery, Ibid., p. 63
6. Frances E.W. Harper, cited by Montgomery, Ibid., p. 41
7. Frances E.W. Harper, cited by Montgomery, Ibid., p. 43
8. Susan B. Anthony, cited by Angela Y. Davis, *Women, Race and Class* (New York: Random House Vintage Edition, 1983) p. 111
9. Frances D. Gage, cited by Montgomery, Op. cit., p. 15
10. Elizabeth C. Stanton, Susan B. Anthony and M.J. Gage, *The History of Woman Suffrage* (New York: Fowler and Wells, 1881) Vol. II, p. 564
11. Frances E.W. Harper, *Iola Leroy or Shadows Uplifted*, Op. cit., pp. 113–114
12. Harriet E. Wilson, *Our Nig* (Boston: Rand and Avery, 1859), pp. 65–66

Yvonne Yarbro-Bejarano

The Image of the Chicana in Teatro

Of all the genres, theater offers the most far-reaching possibilities for the perpetuation or transformation of the stereotypical images of the Chicana. Unlike poetry or fiction, theater is a public, social form, experienced collectively, and as such, it can play a decisive role in shaping the values of a given group. Theater is an important vehicle for questioning or affirming culture in a public forum. In order to assess the image of women in Chicano theater, I have decided to discuss the trajectory of the Teatro de la Esperanza.

El Teatro de la Esperanza

In July of 1971, a group of students and teachers formed El Teatro de la Esperanza (The Theater of Hope). From the beginning, they based themselves in the Chicano community where they continue working out of La Casa de la Raza in Santa Barbara, California. They perform for a bilingual audience primarily in schools and cultural centers throughout the United States. The group is collective in structure and professional in the sense that its members dedicate themselves full time to the work of doing theater. For the past twelve years they have attempted to develop popular political theater as an alternative to the commercial mainstream.

El Teatro de la Esperanza has been relatively successful in refracting the social problems it deals with through the lens of women's experience as well as men's. The group performed its first play, "Guadalupe," from May of 1974 to July of 1975, when it was presented at the Sixth Festival of Chicano Theater in San Antonio, Texas. This play exposes the discrimination and oppression of the Chicano community in the small town of the same name, and gives equal leadership roles to the women in the group of parents who organize a campaign of resistance.

"La víctima"

"La víctima," Esperanza's second work, was performed for the first time in May of 1976 and continues in the active repertory of the group. This play shows how the role of the mother can be handled without falling into stereotypes. The play dramatizes the impact of the discriminatory U.S. immigration policy on a Mexican family. When the family is deported during the Depression, Samuel, the oldest son, is separated from the rest. Raised in the U.S. he eventually becomes an immigration agent, having internalized the values which support the system, yet not without contradiction and conflict. In the climactic scene of the play, Samuel refuses to recognize his true mother and deports her.

It is the mother who sees clearly the extent of his sell-out and confronts him with a series of questions which brings him to an acute awareness of his contradictions. Through her own suffering and that of her other children, she has arrived at a point of dignity, humanity and consciousness equaled by few, if any, other characters in Chicano theater. Besides this key figure, the negative character of Samuel's assimilated, materialistic and social-climbing wife is counterbalanced by the main character's sister, who unlike him, is struggling for the rights of workers, documented and undocumented alike, and his own daughter, who in spite of her class privileges is beginning to question her parents' values and identify with the Chicano Movement.

"Hijos: Once a Family"

Esperanza's third play, "Hijos: Once a Family," was performed from March to November of 1979. This work exhibits a similar strategy in its disposition of male and female characters. The play explores the deterioration of the traditional family in the context of the dominant culture of this society divided into classes. The father, Manuel, exploited in the workplace along with his coworkers, clings to the ideal of The Family. His dream is to save enough money to buy a ranch in Texas, thereby extracting his children from the evil influences of society which he confines to the California milieu, holding up Texas as a pristine ideal, and preserving their values intact. He entrusts his wife with the task of setting aside the savings for the ranch from his meager paycheck. But the children gradually reject the parents' values and adopt those of the middle class to which they aspire.

When Manuel decides to join the strike to protest his unsanitary working conditions, the children rebel, selfishly fearing for their own futures. At this point, his wife reveals to him that there are no savings, that he has been living a fantasy in which the family is supposed to exist outside the pale of social conflict, while she has had to contend on a daily basis with the realities of economic survival. She forces him to see that no island of security exists, not in the family, not in Texas, not anywhere, telling him, "Los problemas son everywhere." Through this confrontation, he is brought to the realization that the only way to safeguard his children's future is to change the very structure which oppresses them all.

While exposing the relation between the crisis in family life and the organization of corporate capitalist society, the play does fall short in its analysis of the problems inherent in the structure of the traditional family itself.

"The Octopus"

The group's fourth play, "The Octopus," debuted in Los Angeles in October of 1980, toured extensively in the Southwest, and was last performed at the 11th Chicano/Latino Theater Festival in San Francisco in September of 1981. "The Octopus" is allegorical/symbolical in form. The Octopus, representing the multinational corporations, owns a Restaurant (the U.S.) in which it exploits the cook and the waiters (workers in the U.S.) and devours all the food which comes from the Village (Third World countries, e.g. El Salvador). When the villagers revolt and cut off the supplies, Johnny Henry, the new waiter in the Restaurant, is sent to recover them.

In the Village he meets an old woman revolutionary, who along with the others is struggling to free the Village from the tentacles of the Octopus. She provides the focus for the second act of the play. In a strategy similar to that of "Hijos" and "La víctima", her fighting spirit and ideological lucidity lead Johnny Henry to an awareness of how the Octopus has him and his co-workers ensnared in a web of lies. While devouring the resources of the Village and growing fat off the work of those in the Restaurant, the Octopus has manipulated the workers' fear and insecurity into distrust and rejection of the villagers' struggle. When Johnny Henry returns to the Restaurant in the third act and challenges the Octopus, it sets up a mock trial in which it accuses him of treason and convinces his co-workers that he is their enemy and should be condemned to death.

Lola, the old revolutionary, has two priceless scenes in the second act which highlight her gumption as well as her political consciousness, both as revolutionary and as a woman. When she and Johnny Henry are jailed in the Village, she enlightens him as to the true nature of the Octopus with a wonderful parable which simply and concisely lays bare the mechanism of exploitation of Third World countries by corporate capitalism. Later, she attempts to warn some young revolutionaries about an ambush and organizes a counter-strategy. They refuse to take her seriously, telling her that if she really wants to help the revolution, she can go home and make them some tortillas. She confronts them with:

> "¡Qué bonito! ¿Esto es lo que queremos poner en poder? ¿Piensan que porque ustedes son los que están peliando que saben todo? Déjame explicarles algo. I won't take too much of your time. Antes de que se enamoraron sus padres yo perdí un hijo y un hermano to this revolución. You say it as if you started it, but hopefully if you can muster up enough brains to blow your noses, you will finish it. You will finish it because I have suffered too long and fought too hard to let ignorant people like you disillusion me and my convictions. It is bad enough that Ratas have come and gone but we still haven't learned that we can be our own most dangerous enemy. Now if you are still willing to fight you will listen to the rest of what I have to say."

This scene has met with enthusiastic response from many in audiences who have had to deal first hand with the contradictions of so-called progressive men who continue to relegate women to a subordinate position in the struggle, to postpone women's issues until some vague moment in the utopian future and to impose oppressive sex roles on them.

Ideological Orientation and the Image of Women

It is not surprising that the group which has consistently challenged the U.S.'s cultural hegemony and outright economic exploitation of poor people and people of color would simultaneously rethink the "natural" superiority of males. From the beginning, Esperanza has defined itself as a political theater and has mounted productions which place the discrimination and exploitation of Chicanos in this country within the larger context of imperialism and corporate capitalisim. It is impossible to seriously confront these questions without realizing that patriarchy is the cornerstone of the system of values generated by these economic interests.

For the same reasons, it is fruitless to discuss the roles women should play in Chicano theater without taking this larger ideological orientation into consideration. It is not a question of merely rejecting certain more "negative" stereotyped roles such as the mother or prostitute and making a mechanical or token substitution of more "positive" ones, such as revolutionary or Adelita with rifles in hand. Esperanza's treatment of the mother in "La víctima" and the wife in "Hijos" suggests that we should begin to focus on how these roles are developed and what the function of the character is in the play as a whole.

In their last play, Esperanza seems to be making an effort to broaden the spectrum of roles for the women in the group. The Octopus, allegorical representation of the web of multinational power, is played by Evelina Fernandez, while Ana Olivares develops her considerable skill as a comic actress in the role of La Rata, general of the U.S.-backed junta in the Village. These roles can be seen as examples of flexibility and exploration when we take the trajectory of Esperanza's theatrical practice into account. In this same play, for example, these two roles are "balanced" by the figure of the old revolutionary.

Central vs. Peripheral Characters

Our concern with the need for our theaters to forge strong, independent female characters and to present social problems in terms of women's experiences as well leads us to ask why the main characters in these plays are always male. The solution to the problems of the male protagonist is not simple. It is not necessarily solved by putting a woman in the central role. Teatro Latino's adaptation of Aristophanes' "Lysistrata," "Liz Estrada," performed during the 11th Chicano/Latino Theater Festival in San Francisco on September 11, 1981, features a female protagonist, but continues to propagate the notion that women's power to change society is limited to influencing their husbands. Besides being indirect, this power is conceived of fundamentally as sexual. Sex becomes a tool by which women manipulate men to get what they want. Although the script attempts to counteract this problem inherited from Aristophanes' comedy by having the women take over the Pentagon and confront the Establishment in other ways, the clearest message the audience takes away from the play is that the women succeed in bringing about certain changes in the barrio by practicing a kind of sexual blackmail on their husbands. Once again we see how the issue of women in theater cannot be separated from the overall analysis of the play or group.

The question concerning main characters goes beyond the fact of being male or female. It is actually part of a larger question of special interest in political theater, namely, what is implied by having a main character at all. There has been much discussion of the idea of the protagonist who incarnates the clash of antagonistic social forces. Instead, people have begun to wonder whether the inclination in theater to create heroes does not imply a tendency to envision social problems as the problems of an extraordinary individual, usually male.

Esperanza seems to be exploring alternatives to this traditional model, to the benefit of their female characterizations. In their first play, "Guadalupe," we search in vain for an individual protagonist. Instead, we are confronted with a group of parents, both male and female, who come together in order to combat the discrimination against their children in the schools of the town. The play was painstakingly put together on the basis of research done in the town on the problems of the community and interviews with the people who had been involved in the events dramatized by the play. When "Guadalupe" was performed in the town of the same name, the people could recognize themselves as the collective protagonist of the play.

In the three works developed after "Guadalupe" — "La víctima," "Hijos" and "The Octopus" — Esperanza seems to have abandoned this approach in a return to the concept of the individual, male main character. But instead of creating heroes, these plays present a series of victims who are weak, contradictory, or otherwise limited in consciousness. Samuel in "La víctima," whose very title announces the new direction of the group, has turned his back on his culture and his class, aspiring to sustain a middle-class lifestyle and internalizing values which allow him to work as an immigration agent. Manuel in "Hijos" lives in a fantasy world in which he nourishes the ideal of the Family untouched by social pressures. Johnny Henry in "The Octopus" is a naive, good-natured type, concerned with staying out of trouble but basically well meaning. He seems to come out of nowhere, agreeing to replace his cousin for one day as a waiter in the Restaurant as a personal favor. In a way, his lack of background and personal definition as a character allow him to assume an off-hand, indifferent attitude toward the Octopus, but at the same time he is easily intimidated and manipulated by the promise of material reward. He more or less accepts the Octopus' version of the situation and agrees to set out on the mission to recover the supplies from the Village and bring them back to the Restaurant. His naiveté permits him to be exploited, and by the second act he is actually working for the interests of the Octopus.

In all three plays, the limited male protagonist is countered by a strong female character who functions as a catalyst in the development of the male characters: Amparo, the mother in "La víctima"; Lola, Manuel's wife in "Hijos"; and Lola, the old revolutionary in "The Octopus." With their superior grasp of reality, they either succeed in transforming the consciousness of the male protagonist or at least bring their contradictions to the point of maximum tension. In any case, all three males are ultimately victims. Samuel, in the process of dehumanizing others, has become dehumanized himself. The play ends with a nightmare in which he confronts the full meaning of his betrayal of mother, class and culture. Manuel dies in the moment in which he realizes the connection between his family and his exploitation as a worker. Johnny Henry is condemned to death for his new-found political consciousness by his own co-workers.

The ultimate effect of these plays is not pessimistic, however, in part due to the existence of viable struggles represented in other characters, usually female, and especially due to the fact that the alternative of positive action transcends the boundaries of the play and is handed over to the spectators in the form of a choice.

Dialogue on Sexism

Since "The Octopus," Esperanza has developed and toured a musical show, "La muerte viene cantando" ("Death Comes Singing"). This piece, first performed in April of 1983 and still in the repertory, works within the Chicano theater tradition of dramatizing *corridos* (popular songs from the oral ballad tradition) and using *calaveras* (skeletons) as the dominant visual image projected by the actors and actresses. But whereas Luis Valdez, in his commercial hit *Corridos*, has drawn fire for the negative treatment of women, Esperanza chose texts which portray Chicanas and Latinas as active participants in history. One *corrido* tells the story of a peasant woman who avenges her rape and the murder of her brother with her military abductor's own pistol. Other numbers celebrate the role of women in the Mexican and Nicaraguan revolutions. One particularly eloquent piece dramatizes Domitila's speech to a middle-class woman who has addressed her as "sister" in an appeal for solidarity on the basis of their sex. Domitila's response captured the position of many Chicanas who insist on the recognition of class differences in their definition of feminism.

In the future, we can expect Esperanza to continue to provide us with serious dialogue on sexism with *teatro* organizations as well as ground-breaking roles for women in their plays.

Kathleen Shaye Hill

The Yellow Dress

This is an excerpt from my novel-in-progress. The book focuses on the women of a Klamath family and their struggle to maintain their Indian/tribal/familial identity during the 1970s. This struggle is exacerbated by the unique political situation of the Klamaths — victims of the Federal Government's assimilationist policies which, during the 1950s, were developed explicitly to erode tribalism and eventually left us without a reservation.

The breeze was coming from the north — all the way home Jannette had been able to smell the pine trees and sage up towards what had once been the reservation, the Old Lands. The sun had been out only long enough to take off the night chill by the time she finished her walk home. On reaching the front yard, she kicked off her shoes and stood barefoot in a bunch of dew-covered crabgrass, letting the coolness soothe her blistered feet.

The whole distance she'd been wondering if there would be time to recuperate before facing the Old Lady. The way she had it figured, RoseMary would be asleep another half an hour or so. That is, if she hadn't waited up all night.

As she crossed the creaking boards of the front porch without seeing the Old Lady's small brown face peeking out from beside the white shades in the living room window, she was pretty sure she had made it home free. At least for a little while. She inched the door open, thankful her mother never bothered to use the lock on it. There was no use walking into a head-on collision with her.

Seeing for sure that RoseMary wasn't yet up, Jannette got a little braver, brave enough to let loose a heavy sigh, then head into the bathroom. She ran a sinkful of cold water and put her yellow dress into it, making sure that all of the bloody spots were completely submerged. Damn. It was the only summer dress she owned, the first new dress she had gotten in the three years since Randy's funeral and here it was, blood-stained, while both of those ugly black dresses hanging in the closet still looked brand new. Wasn't that life.

Jannette turned the shower on and stepped into it, letting the warm water ease over her just long enough to take some of the ache away, then turned it colder, colder, colder until her whole body went numb. It was time to check out the consequences of last night; she couldn't put it off any longer. Abruptly, she turned the water off, wrapped herself in a towel and looked into the medicine chest mirror over the sink. God. How was she going to explain this one to the Old Lady? She winced at the thought and a sharp pain shot through her left cheekbone. Was it broken or just cut again?

Maybe she could get rid of some of the swelling with ice. Jannette put her robe on and crept into the kitchen to get out a couple of cubes. She knew she couldn't do anything about the bruises. But, if she could just get rid of a few of those puffy, swollen spots on her forehead and cheek before RoseMary got up it might make the whole morning go a little easier. Shit. Sometimes it seemed like the questions were harder to take than the beatings themselves. She knew darn well what the first question would be. That was one thing that never changed. Same as always, the Old Lady would eat her breakfast, rock in the damned chair for a minute or two, look at the rug on the floor, then — slowly — ask, "Did one of those white men beat you up?"

As far as Jannette could see, there wasn't any sense to a question like that. Sometimes the Old Lady's ignorance really showed. Ask any woman who'd been knocked around a time or two. Didn't make much difference what color that fist was — when it came crashing down, all that mattered was the punch behind it. One look at her and the Old Lady ought to know that *who* did it wasn't exactly number one priority right now.

For a few minutes Jannette kicked around the idea of going to bed. Sure as hell'd make more sense than waiting around for a fight. But she'd tried that before. Even an extra hour of sleep wasn't worth the tossing and turning she did when she knew her mother had gone without breakfast. Somebody had to fix the Old Lady's meals and with her brother, Randy, dead and Jack up there in the State Pen it didn't take a genius to guess who. Sometimes she wondered why RoseMary didn't hire herself some dependable outside help with the money she must have gotten from selling the family's ranch.

She tossed what was left of the ice cubes into the sink. Hell with it, she decided as she headed to the back door, might as well wonder in one hand and spit in the other. No use wasting her time thinking about all that stuff now. No matter what excuse she came up with — and she'd considered them all — she knew damn well she'd end up fixing breakfast for her mother. Figuring she might as well enjoy the wait, Jannette left the wooden door open, lit a Winston and sat down in the sunshine on the cool cement step of the back porch. It was going to be a hot one today.

It couldn't have been more than fifteen minutes before she heard the toilet flush. She debated the situation — should she go on in now and get it over with or hang around the kitchen until breakfast was ready?

Shit. Better enjoy the distance while she had it. There really wasn't any use in getting the Old Lady all fired up any sooner than necessary.

When she went back into the kitchen, Jannette poured herself a cup of coffee and pulled out another cigarette before getting the trout and eggs from the refrigerator. As she tapped the end of the cigarette on the counter, she could feel herself slowing down, stretching each of the sixty seconds of every minute for its full worth. RoseMary must be in the living room by now.

Oh, God. The dress! Goddamn it! She'd left the dress in the sink. Well — the Old Lady would know by now that something was up.

She dipped the fish, one side then the other, into the flour canister then into the cast iron skillet of sizzling oleo. What now? Should she go on in and face the music? Should she bring it up first or let RoseMary? If she brought it up first, maybe that would put her on the defensive. Shoot. When it came right down to it, it wasn't any of the Old Lady's damned business anyway.

What was the deal with old people? she wondered. They spent half a lifetime raising you to mind your own business then spent the other half butting into everyone else's. Criminy. Here she was, thirty-three years old and shaking in her boots about what her mommy was going to say!

Jannette flipped the fish over with the spatula, spattering grease all over the stove top, cracked the eggs into the other pan and pulled a clean plate and cup from the cupboard, slamming the doors. She'd sure as hell do what she wanted, when she wanted, with whoever she wanted! She cooked and straightened up the house in exchange for a private bedroom — that little one room shack out back — a few dollars, and a meal now and then, and that was all she owed the Old Lady. Besides that, she was the one doing the Old Lady a favor. If it wasn't for her, RoseMary would be trapped in this dumpy little house with nothing for company but dustballs and a broken down t.v. So, just who did she think she was, carrying on like some old white church lady? Seemed like a grown-up woman ought to be able to have a good time if she got the urge. That was it. She'd made up her mind and this time she wasn't going to take any baloney from that crippled old woman. If she didn't like the way Jannette chose to live her life, that was her problem. A daughter's obligations had limits, just like everyone else's.

With that last thought, she dumped the coffee into the cup, the eggs and fish onto the plate, retied the belt of her bathrobe and headed through the hall to the living room.

Her mother jumped a little when she entered the living room. Served the Old Lady right. Damned if she was going to tippy-toe around like a naughty little schoolgirl every time she spent the night partying.

Jannette lit another cigarette and watched in silence as Rose-Mary ate. Old people ate so funny. Little tiny bites just like a baby. She was getting tired of the old woman taking her for granted. Like just now for instance — hadn't even bothered to say thank you when she'd handed her the plate. Used to be, she'd at least say thank you. Maybe she was pouting. She always pouted when she didn't get her way, when Jannette had a good time. Just sat there like she thought she was an old wooden Indian or something. Hmph. Didn't look like any wooden Indian Jannette had ever seen.

RoseMary finished her breakfast, then sat perfectly still. It was only the rise and fall of her chest that gave evidence of life. She was so small and wrinkled that she hardly looked real at all. She looked like some kind of foreigner with that kerchief on her head. Why did she wear that stupid thing all the time, anyway? Jannette took out another Winston and started blowing smoke rings. One last cigarette and it was off to bed.

It was strange that the Old Lady hadn't said anything yet. She usually started in soon as she finished the last biteful of food. But this morning, the silence in the house was so complete that Jannette could hear the neighbor lady across the street call out a goodbye to her husband, the car salesman.

Every now and then, she would catch the Old Lady looking up at her, but she'd shoot her a stern look and RoseMary would turn her face back down toward the floor. If I can just keep this up, Jannette figured, she won't go butting in with her usual questions.

● ● ●

RoseMary didn't know how much longer she could wait. Maybe if she was real careful about how she put it, Jannette wouldn't get so mad this time.

Well, one thing was sure, things couldn't go on like this. If Jannette didn't get any sleep, she'd be grouchy. If she was grouchy, then she'd go out and drink too much again. And if she kept doing that, she'd die pretty soon just like so many of her generation had. RoseMary cleared her throat and looked up at her daughter one more time. It wasn't until that moment, with Jannette's head tipped back to make the smoke rings, that RoseMary saw the side of her face. Her stomach got sick. Oh, no, she felt so sick. . . . Maybe an Indian man beat her up. Probably that Sioux man she'd been talking about. Maybe even a Klamath man who found out where she got that fancy yellow dress. But what if it had been that white man she'd been seeing lately? Now, that was scary. When an Indian man beat up an Indian woman, it was usually because he was drunk or mad. When a white man beat up an Indian woman, it seemed like it was because he hated her. Or because he hated all Indians. Like that guard at the B.I.A. school. How many Indian girls did he beat up before he finally killed that one and they retired him?

The old woman knew she would be taking a big chance, asking that question again, but if she didn't ask she wouldn't know the answer. Jannette never volunteered to tell her anything. What little RoseMary did know, she usually learned by overhearing Jannette talking on the telephone. Like about that pretty little yellow dress soaking in the bathroom sink. Sure thing she wouldn't have known that some white man had given her daughter that yellow dress if Jannette hadn't been so anxious to call around and brag about it to her girlfriends.

RoseMary began to rock and cleared her throat a second time. She noticed the muscles in her daughter's neck and jaw tighten, then flinch, as if it hurt that cut, bruised spot under her hair. Well, she'd gone this far, no use putting it off now.

"Did one of those white men beat you up last night?" RoseMary asked.

There was no answer.

"I said to you: did one of those white men beat you up last night?"

Jannette finally turned around, facing her directly — "What's it to you?"

"There is blood all over your new dress. I saw it in the sink. It has blood all over it," RoseMary said.

"So? What do you care? What difference does it make to you?

Aren't you glad? I thought you'd be real glad it's ruined, seeings as you never liked it in the first place."

"That's not true," RoseMary said. "I like it. I told you it was pretty. I just don't think a man should give clothes to a woman he's not a relative to. Besides . . . there is blood all over it."

"So what?"

"So, did that white man beat you up? That one that gave you that dress?"

"Why don't you just mind your own goddamned business, Old Lady? What do you know about life anyway? What do you know about anything, anyway?"

"I know better than to spend time with white people who don't like me and that might maybe beat me up."

"Well . . . la-tee-dah. If you know so *damned* much," here Jannette paused, letting the cussword sink in, ". . . if you're so smart, how come you never learned your own lesson? You know, the one you harped on me about, the one that goes 'mind your own business'?"

"Do you forget that you are my daughter—my only daughter? Do you forget that it is the duty of a mother to watch out for her daughter? Protect her? Do you forget everything I ever tried to teach you?"

"Just stop it!" Jannette snapped. "I'm sick and tired of listening to all that old-fashioned crap! Do *you* forget that I'm an adult? If I had kids, I'd sure as hell know better than to butt into their business every time they took a little turn off the straight and narrow!"

RoseMary turned her face back toward the rug, her voice even lower than usual, almost a whisper, "And do you, my only daughter, forget even that you do have children?"

Jannette opened her mouth, but the sound stayed in. Her jaw began to quiver, but there was still nothing coming out. Finally, she just said, "Damn you," then turned on her heel and headed back down the hall toward the kitchen.

RoseMary could hear the back screen-door bounce loudly once, then in little echoing sounds come gradually to a standstill as her daughter went to the bedroom out back. It was hard to sit with herself now: who had she become, that she could have been so mean to her own daughter? To anything but those little ones Jannette had a thick skin. She couldn't stand to think about those babies. Even RoseMary found it hard to think about the grandchildren who were almost grown without even knowing her. Another bunch of Klamath kids who didn't know their own people. How could they ever know what it really meant to be an Indian—to be a

Klamath — out there in the world like that, when even the young people here at home found it so hard?

She had really done it this time. Sure thing Jannette would go out drinking again tonight, after her nap . . . yellow dress or no yellow dress.

Sure thing.

Julia Boyd

Something Ain't Right

Just the other day I was talking on the phone to my friend Beth. Now Beth had called me and she was real upset, yelling and screaming, just carrying on. She was uptight because the Equal Rights Amendment didn't pass. She was talking about how I should be upset, too, because this E.R.A. is just as much for Black women as it is for white women. Now what I didn't tell Beth, but what I'm thinking is how in the hell can I be upset about something called E.R.A. when I got to think up a way to scrape together enough money to pay my rent, which is a month behind. I mean if this woman really wanted to get my attention, all she would have to do was tell me how I could come across some coins, so I'd have a roof over my head for another month. I mean, now really, some folks just get outlandish in their request for my sympathy!

As Beth proceeds to tell me how I shouldn't be bitter about what's happened in the past, I roll my eyes to the ceiling and switch the phone to my good ear. I can tell by her voice that she's getting ready to launch into one of her lectures about how folks got to stick together and how we're all sisters under the skin. I don't know about her, but the only thing under my skin right now is nerves, and Beth don't realize it but she's touching on my last one right about now. She wants me to march with the local women's group on Saturday, down to the City Hall for a protest. Now I have told that woman once that I did my marching in the 60s, and besides, the last time I used my combat boots was to throw one at the neighbor's dog at 5 o'clock in the morning. This woman just never gives up. Before I can get a word in edgewise, she tells me that she's gotta go because it's time for her to pick up her son Randy from pre-school.

As I hung up the phone, I thought about Beth and her so-called dedication to the movement. Here she was preaching to me about equal rights, movements and shit, but she's living in a condo, driving a 280Z and selling real estate for a living. Here I am living in the projects, cruising in Red Death and slaving at the Center. Sure she's divorced and a single parent, but her Ex, as she likes to call him, sends her child support payments every month. My Old Man disappeared the same day the rabbit died; and unless his daddy's Uncle Sam, the last time I got a check for support it was signed by the Treasurer of the United States.

I mean something ain't right. It's not that I'm against Women's Lib and all that stuff, but how come in the 60s when I was marching for those very same rights, nobody paid us any attention but the 6 o'clock news. Even then it wasn't good coverage, or newsworthy as they say, unless we were singing hymns from behind bars.

I guess I can understand Beth's being upset about this E.R.A. thing because she's white, and I ought to know by now that white women have a thing about wanting their so-called rights. But what they fail to recognize is that I was born fighting for my rights, and no E.R.A. or any other R.A. is going to make one hill of beans to me if I don't have a roof over my head.

Beth's been working herself up into a tailspin for the past couple of years over the E.R.A. She calls herself schooling me about this whole political scene, explaining how if this E.R.A. passes it will mean better jobs and equal pay for women. Here she comes telling me how this amendment will open up more opportunities for women. Most of the time I don't say anything. I just sit and listen to her spout off. But in the back of my mind I'm thinking, well where was this E.R.A. when Black folks were getting lynched and run out of the South? I mean, now really! If she wanted to talk about being equal, where was this so-called E.R.A. when my mama was scrubbing her mama's floors for $3.00 a week and carfare, along with all the leftover scraps from the table? Even at that she didn't bring home none of the good stuff, like meat.

Beth is always telling me how women are oppressed and overlooked in the world. Funny thing is she never talks about oppression until she can't get what she wants. Me, I've known about oppression for a long time. Hell, you can't be Black or any other color without dealing with The Man. Folks come along, think up a fancy name for something and expect a body to buy into it lock, stock and barrel. Wanting equal rights is yesterday's news for me and other Black women, and jumping on the bandwagon behind a white woman hollering to get her equal rights wouldn't help my cause any. Hell, they forget we Black Women built that wagon they're riding on, and I'll be damned if I'm going to push the wagon too.

Debra C. Earling

Perma Red

She had been walking on the highway for almost an hour. Last night's liquor was now just a cotton-dry whisper on her thick tongue, a faint buzz somewhere behind her head. The bastard had let her off outside of Ravalli on Highway 93, and now nearly an hour later, she was nowhere closer to Perma. The armholes of her blouse were tight and wet. The stiff blouse strained across her breast and had rubbed her nipples raw.

Her stomach rumbled. "No," she groaned. She looked for privacy. A lonely bush, a few scrub trees, sage, weeds, and dry grass. Rattlers? She looked to the pine trees a hundred yards or so further. "Hell with it," she said and ducked behind the nearest bush. When Louise stepped back onto the road the heavy August sun was clearing the Mission Range. Her knees felt a little weak but she was now ready to walk a serious mile or two. A breeze cooled the sweat on her back and fluttered her thin skirt. She felt the hem wet on her calves and shivered. Although she tried to walk fast, she felt as if she were being pulled down. Each landmark she set her sights on remained distant, unobtainable. She shifted her gaze to the blonde hills.

The stiff grass rustled in the breeze. A gust of wind rattled the dry weeds, whirled a tumbleweed and threw a sheet prickle of dust up her legs. Grit stung her eyes. She stopped on the road's shoulder and watched the small whirlwind gather speed, twirling leaves, small twigs, powder dust. Under its path, thin rows of cheat grass collapsed like brittle sticks. She stood transfixed and watched until the swirling talcum dust disappeared in a steady cross-wind, becoming a faint wisp, a tendril of smoke, thin air.

Her grandmother believed whirlwinds were the souls of the dead, departing, becoming sky. Spirit winds. Louise had never really believed this. Now she swallowed a growing desire to run . She forced herself to walk slowly, but little by little, she began to quicken her pace.

She heard the hollow wind sound of an approaching car. She lifted her thumb, but the car swerved a perfect half moon to avoid her and whipped down the road. A glint of chrome and it disappeared over a hillswell. She raised a slender hand to her brow and blinked at the sun. It wasn't even close to noon and already the road was soft beneath her feet. She wasn't worried though; someone would pick her up, someone whom she knew and she would sit redfaced and silent on the way back home, wishing she had made it to Missoula, or Wallace, anywhere, off this reservation. The thought chewed her pride. This time it'd be different — she'd walk all the bitchin' way home. She stiffened her knees and her heart became her drumbeat homeward.

The shallow drone of an occasional passing car eased the monotony of the fields' humming. She listened to the steady flickering tick of the grasshopper and tried to block the image of her mother's fever-swollen face. She tried to think up an excuse for last night's drunk. But she knew excuses didn't matter now. She had come up with convincing alibis in the past. And Grandma would listen intently, nod politely, and excuse her. She would feel a little guilty at first, but later she would feel smug. But she was never sure she had fooled the old woman, only pride made her hold onto the thought that she had.

"Hey Louise! Red! Want a ride?" Behind her, grinning — cousin Victor hung out the window of his rusty '32 Ford pick-up. A slow cloud of dust billowed past her. He squinted at her, chewing on a tooth pick. His black-gray hair was butch block, bristled like a wire brush. Occasionally, he would get a crew-cut and when it grew out it made his head look square. He was wearing the maroon shirt he always wore, rolled up past his forearms, with a white tee shirt underneath. He looked hot.

Louise said nothing, walked to the passenger side and yanked on the door. Victor tried to roll down the window but it stuck. He yelled at her through the window crack. "Door don't open." He gestured with his fingers. "Gotta come around on my side." Louise noticed again the thin white scar that split his upper lip. It occurred to her that white men didn't have scars. He climbed out of the truck. And Louise crawled in. The dull leather seats were hot and she sat close to the passenger door on a seat rip that was sharp. It snagged her skirt.

The truck pulled out on the road and picked up speed until the window crack whistled and the stick shift vibrated. Victor spit out his toothpick. "Whew," he said, "you smell like a white woman. Where you been?" Louise folded her arms across her sore breasts and looked at the dashboard. A bumper sticker sealed off the jockey box. She read its faded letters: 'Pray For Me, I Drive Highway '93.''

"Got any booze?" she said. He reached across her and pulled out a half-empty quart of beer. The bent bottle cap had been jammed back on and Louise pulled it off with her fingers. She took a long, easy swig of the flat warm beer and passed it to Victor. He chugged a few swallows. "Taste like dog piss!" he coughed.

"I wouldn't know," Louise said and gulped a quick swallow, then recapped it with her fist. She put the bottle between her legs. The seat poked her thighs.

"What'd you do to your hair, kid? It looks faded somehow."

"Got any gum?" she said.

He reached into his pocket, pulled out a stick of clove gum and tossed it in her lap. Last month she had heard you could lighten your hair with peroxide and water, so she had tried it. She stared out the window. "I like it," she mumbled and wiped her wet palms on her knees. Louise watched the clear shadow of a cloud as it moved over the hills. And it seemed to her that the hills were sleeping. She thought of her mother laying still beneath the clouds in the white heat of the day.

He spoke softly. "I heard Annie's been sick. Aunt Susy was up to your Grandma's house last night." Louise chewed the cuticle on her left thumb and busied herself smoothing her skirt. She looked at her brown shoes but said nothing. Her mother had been sick for only a week, but it was a different sickness. A sickness that pulled the muscles behind her eyes as tight as a blind strap and let go.

Now, every night Grandma listened for the owl and burned the thin strands of Annie's hair in the cook-stove. She also kept a tireless eye on Annie's lonely clothing flapping on the line. If she left her post she would call Louise to stand watch — so neither Annie nor her possessions were ever left alone.

Louise listened to the sound of the tires on the road and re-opened the beer. "Want a chug?" she pointed the bottle toward Victor. He shook his head. The truck hit a bump and beer splattered his lap. She gulped the rest, leaned over and tossed the bottle out his window. She heard a distant tinkle as it hit the ground.

"Aunt Susy says it's bad medicine." He looked at her.

"What?"

She had come from Hot Springs, the old medicine woman. Even in the bright sun, her clothes were black as the crows' wings. Louise remembered that the rattlesnakes buzzed her arrival. Rattlesnakes were blind this time of year. They hid in the grass with milk-white eyes.

They struck at anything that moved.

"What?"

"Your mother's sickness."

"I don't know." She felt as if a cold, wet hand had just been placed at the base of her spine. She choked a gag.

Victor changed the subject. "Been a bad spell this summer. Road's too hot, even for snakes. You're lucky you have that spring."

Louise nodded, but said nothing.

The spring's creek was a slow mud trickle thick as blood. Grandma had milked the old cow for Annie and sent Louise down to the spring with a small jar of body-warm milk. The spring pool still bubbled, but it had receded and large mosquitos swarmed the cracked clay banks. Louise had slipped the jar in an old stocking and put it in the creek. For an hour she had sat holding onto the sock, slapping blood fat mosquitos.

They were slowing coming into Dixon. Victor shifted into second and the truck whined down. A few cars were parked at the Dixon Bar. Now it was early afternoon and shadows were short. A dirt gray dog slept in the shade of the Dixon Bar.

The milk was cool and sweet when they put it to her lips, but it dribbled through her hot yellow teeth and scummed the inside of her cheeks like phlegm; a gray paste too thick to swallow. Her ragged fingernails, thin and dry as paper.

"This sure is one hell of a town," Victor said. Louise looked over at the Dixon Bar and could see only darkness behind the ragged screen door. She placed her hand to the back of her neck and thought of sleep. Victor scuffed the palm of his hand over his hair and sighed. As they drove out of Dixon Louise noticed a small boy was playing near the edge of town. Louise turned to look back. A slow cloud of dust was passing over a few gray shingle houses built squat on the ground. The small boy had stopped playing. She saw him raise his hand as if to wave but he cupped his hand above his eyes then lifted his dark face to the sun.

Louise slumped back in the seat and crossed her arms. As she saw her Grandma's house in the distance she sat up suddenly and tugged at her door handle. "Let me out here, Victor." He started to protest but slowed down the truck and let her out. She stood squinting on the roadside and watched until Victor's pickup turned the first highway bend and slipped beyond the hill.

The weathered house stood among the weeds. Near the highway was a marshy stretch, thick with fuzzy cattails and cawing magpies. The rocky terrain of Grandma's land provided a haven for field snakes and rattlers. Louise walked slowly up to the house. She adjusted her skirt and wiped her mouth on the back of her hand.

For a while she stood, stoneblind and blinking in the doorway. She leaned into the queer hot darkness, straining to see. Her eyes gathered the dark room slowly, one inch at a time. Heavy blankets, smelling like singed hair hid the windows and suffocated the afternoon sun. Here and there pinholes of light poked the walls, illuminating golden particles of dust.

In the dim light, she saw the still shadow of Grandma standing near the cook-stove. Grandma opened the cast iron stove drawer and fanned the flames. Her face was washed with yellow light. She threw something into the flames and shut the drawer. Louise watched a thin flicker of fire lick the round edge of the stove lid and her nostrils were filled with the smell of burning sweet grass. Grandma pulled another grass braid from her deep pocket and touched it to the stove top. An orange flame smoked the withering grass. Grandma carried the smoking medicine to the bedroom where Annie lay. The door closed behind her with a quiet click. Louise clasped her hands to keep her fingers from trembling. And sat down in the sleepy heat and waited.

Annie's wake was held at Aunt Susy's house. The first day of the wake Louise waited outside of the small house. For a while she hid in the root cellar and listened to the sound of her heart. That evening Louise stood behind the pine tree in Aunt Susy's front yard. She cupped her hands to her ribs and watched the people who came to visit her mother for the last time. Even outside she could hear them praying. Sometimes she could hear them laughing and joking. And when they cried, Louise would sit on the porch and listen to the wind moving through the cheat grass.

Aunt Susy came out on the porch to sit beside her once. She had reached over and touched Louise's hand. Louise had looked at her in the darkness and thought the old woman's skin resembled the pickled tavern sausages at the Perma Bar. The old woman seemed small to Louise now. When Louise was a little girl she had been afraid of Aunt Susy. The old woman had a wizened hawk-face and a large dowager's hump. She always wore black garments. And some of her dresses had sleeves short enough to reveal the loose, olive flesh of her inner arms. Once Louise mentioned her Aunt Susy's skin color to Grandma. "Too much green tea," Grandma had said.

For three days and three nights they prayed for Annie. Louise watched Grandma in the kitchen sifting flour for fry bread. Louise could see the mouse turds like hard raisins grate the bottom of the sifter. Grandma would toss them out, scoop up another cup and dump it in the sifter.

Louise looked into the living room where her mother lay propped in a wooden box. She clenched her skirt up tight in her fists and stood still. "Go to her," Grandma said. Louise did not move for a moment. "Go on," her grandmother said. Louise walked slowly toward her mother. The candles flickered up on Annie's delicate, waxen face. Annie's slender hands had been folded carefully across her bosom.

And Louise noticed that her mother's hands were still and dark. For a long time Louise gazed upon her, looking for signs of life. Twice, she saw her chest expand, gathering air. But looking again, it seemed to Louise that she had never seen anything so motionless. Even dust moved in the wind. And sometimes rocks seemed to shimmer in the heat. But her mother's stillness was uncomfortable to her. Louise passed her hand over her mother's face but did not touch her.

Louise looked above the casket where, haphazardly tacked on the gray wall, were pictures that Aunt Susy had cut out of magazines and catalogues. Fashion models smiled from the windows of their chauffeured cars. Hawaiian girls waved from a tropical paradise. Happy families sat down to dine in their immaculate kitchens.

Friends and relatives began to pray. Louise looked at their faces. Every face seemed distorted to her; continually changed by the candlelights' flickering. It seemed to Louise that they looked at her mother as though she were far away. Their eyes seemed vague and distant to her. Nervous fingers twisted rosaries. Some sang softly, almost inaudibly. Their chants became a low drone that buzzed like the hot fields. She looked at her grandmother in the kitchen. Louise wondered what caused this dark sadness. It seemed she had felt this way for a long time. Louise slipped out the door without a goodbye.

Louise returned home the next morning before the heat could dry the root-wet fields. She saw Victor's gray Ford parked out back. She held her breath, but she soon realized they had left sometime before.

When she opened the back door she called to her grandmother. She looked at the half empty coffee cups on the table. She sat down in the quiet kitchen; her skull felt thin as an eggshell. A meadowlark sang outside the window and she thought it was a lonely sound. She thought a while and went outside. Maybe Victor had left his keys in the truck. She peered in the window. No keys in the ignition. She opened the door and checked under the mat. She found an old gray key. She wondered if it would work.

The truck picked up speed, faster and faster, until the seats lurched and the rusted coil springs screeched with the rhythmic jar of the road's many potholes. Dust motes billowed behind the truck. Louise pressed the accelerator to the floor and gripped the steering wheel. The road gave way to a series of sharp bends that ended in a roller coaster hill. She sighed as the road gradually sloped to a straight tractor road.

Louise could see the small crowd at the burial ground so she began to slow down. She pulled the truck off on the roadside. Her tight chest felt empty and she was breathing hard. Louise rolled the window down and gulped a breath of air. She pressed her forehead to the steering wheel. Over the field, the wind carried the old songs. A warm breeze touched her damp hair. Louise looked over at the people gathered around the grave; eight or nine people she had known all her life. Grandma's red shawl flapped in the hot wind. She saw that all of them were wearing their best clothes. Victor stood close to Grandma in his stiff white shirt.

Louise twisted the mirror round so she could look at her face. In the sunlight she could see that the red color of her hair did not match her dark skin. She looked for something to cover her head. On the floor was an old bandana that Victor used to stuff the window crack. Carefully she tied the scarf over her hair. Louise looked at herself once more and slowly climbed out of the truck. She left the truck door open and walked a little closer. She waited until the small crowd departed. "Grandma?" she called. Grandma and Victor looked up at Louise.

"I'll meet you both at the truck," he said.

Louise moved slowly toward Grandma. "I know, Honey," Grandma said. "It's going to be fine."

Grandma lifted her palms to the sky and chanted in Salish. Her chant became a slow, meandering song that made Louise very sad. She sang to a part of Louise that was lonesome.

Dorothy Laigo Cordova

Pinays — Filipinas in America

Filipinas in America, born of a culture with roots in both Spanish colonialism and Pacific Island influences, have been strong working and family women. Though some came from a middle or upper-class background, leaving the domestic nest for promises of riches through education and work in America, they faced no easy life upon landing on these shores.

Through the lives of Filipinas who came to America during the Depression, we learn of a shared sense of educational purpose, family solidarity and community support indicative of a tightly knit Filipino community which still is growing rapidly in the Northwest.

The Philippines became part of the United States when Spain sold its former colony for $20,000,000 in the 1898 Treaty of Paris, which ended the Spanish-American War and removed Spain as a colonial power. Millions of Filipinos who had earlier welcomed the United States as an ally against the tyranny of Spain felt betrayed by the terms of the treaty. The Philippine Insurrection was a militant protest against the lack of independent nation status and lasted for years. After the U.S. quelled the insurrection by superior weaponry, it began the "Americanization" of the Philippines.

Filipinos became wards of the United States. As nationals they were allowed to come to this country as long as they had the price of their boat ticket. This policy lasted until the passage of the Tydings–McDuffie Act in 1934 which restricted the entry of Filipinos into the U.S. to a mere 50 people per year. The Act also changed the status of Filipinos from American nationals to "alien immigrants."

In this sketch of three Pinays — Filipina women — we focus on women who came to America during the period after the Spanish-American War and before the enactment of the Tydings–McDuffie Act. Contrary to popular conception, Filipinas during this time were not denied the right to come to America. Lack of funds or an adequate chaperone were usually the principal restrictions.

These three individuals came from different parts of the Philippines. Two arrived during the late '20s — one a nurse who sought employment first in the Midwest and then in New York before settling in Seattle; the other a school teacher who never finished the education she sought. The third came in the early '30s — a high-spirited teenager taking advantage of the educational opportunity offered by an uncle.

All three women learned that life in America during the Depression was not easy for anyone — much less for people of color. At times acting as the heads of their families, these women lovingly raised children, cared for relatives and preserved cultural traditions while working one, two, and even three jobs. Their stories are not unique, but are cherished as important parts of a history of Filipinas in America which must never be lost.

With recently relaxed immigration laws, as well as the political and economic unrest in the Philippines, Filipinos are today among the fastest-growing groups of Asian/Pacific Islanders in America. Population figures for Filipinos in the U.S. rose from about 343,000 in 1970 to almost 775,000 in 1980. In Washington State, the numbers rose from about 11,500 in 1970 to almost 25,000 in 1980.

As third- and fourth-generations of Filipino-Americans assimilate into mainstream American society and "culture," some are renewing cultural ties with their Filipino traditions.

Filipinas in America now make strides as lawyers, teachers and professional women, but never forget the hard work and discrimination early Filipina newcomers faced — and which the new contemporary counterparts, today's immigrants, still face in terms of racial, gender and economic oppression.

The following accounts were taken from interviews conducted by two oral history projects — The Washington State Oral/Aural History Program (1974–1977), and the Demonstration Project for Asian Americans/Filipino Oral History Project (1980–1982). In these excerpts, the women describe their arrival and life in the Pacific Northwest fifty to sixty years ago.

Felicidad Espiritu Acena

"I was working in the Zamboanga General Hospital as a nurse . . . I applied in Cleveland, Ohio, as a nurse, and my friend, Miss Nonacedo came with me. . . . So we came September on the *Empress of Russia* . . . a steam boat."

Many Filipino women who came to the United States during the '20s and '30s intended to further their education or their careers. One of those intent on a career was Felicidad Espiritu Acena, who was born in 1892 in Vigan, Ilocos Sur. She came to America in 1926 when she was thirty-four years old. Her family did not encourage her to come to America. Her mother wanted her to work as a nurse in Zamboanga, but Felicidad wanted to see the United States.

> "Oh, I remember that when we were in the boat, there were twenty-seven Filipinos in the steerage. We had a cabin in second class. We were only two (women) there. So, we enjoy them . . . and there were Filipino musicians on that boat . . . was very good."

Her port of entry was Victoria, B.C. From there she and Miss Nonacedo continued their journey on the Canadian Railroad. They stopped in North Dakota and went to Cleveland on another train. They arrived in Cleveland in October, 1926.

They remained for six months, then moved to New York to apply for positions in the Jewish Hospital in Brooklyn where Felicidad and her friend obtained jobs. The two women were treated well in the hospitals, but experienced some problems of discrimination outside work.

Nurses in those days worked long hours — up to twelve hours a day. However, they received free room and board in the nurses' residence. Staff members enjoyed additional side benefits at Jewish Hospital — for example, the nurses often received gifts from patients who were being discharged.

She remained in Brooklyn until 1931. She passed the nurses' examination and was registered in New York State. In October, 1931, she came to Seattle to join her husband, Eladio Acena, who had conducted a long-distance courtship for several years.

> "We were married in New York. You know, a civil (marriage), something like that. And we celebrated in the Cathedral here in Seattle."

Felicidad found she could not find work in Seattle as a nurse; it was the Depression and there were few jobs. She also did not have her Washington State nursing license, so she went to the University of Washington to take additional courses in nursing at the same time she attended Broadway High School to complete her high school studies. (It was not mandatory then to complete high school in order to study nursing. She had begun her nursing studies while still a high school sophomore in the Philippines.)

In addition to completing her studies, she gave birth to a son,

Albert. She also opened her home to boarders.

> "We cook for them and then they come and eat. They said they will pay you after Alaska, but they never come and pay. It's good that Laddy (her husband) had that job there."

Her husband had come to the United States to study medicine, but he and a brother set aside their own ambitions to finance their sister's medical studies.

> "You know, Laddy was always working in that General Hospital all the time because he was always in the operating room, assisting those doctors there . . . he was a male nurse."

Felicidad continued to work as a nurse during World War II. In 1946, her husband died and she became the sole support for her son. She remarried a distant relative of her late husband and became the head of her extended family. During holidays she would be host to relatives, in-laws, neighbors from Vigan and other friends.

Eventually she retired. Her son, Albert, became the first Filipino-American in Washington to receive a doctorate degree and now teaches history at the College of San Mateo in California. She remained an active member of the Third Order of St. Francis until the end of her life. Felicidad died in 1979, outliving two husbands.

Bibiana Montante Laigo Castillano

> "My father talked of my coming to America and asked me if I wished to go. I was teaching . . . Well, thinking about the salary that the Filipino (teachers) were receiving over there (Philippines), I jumped at the chance — I was so pleased. I was twenty-four then. My father said, 'It's not nice for you to go alone, so you'd better go with your brother James. . . . So I was so happy and here we come. And we rode on . . . *The President Grant* . . . Well, I got seasick. I'd never rode on a boat before, except a little one . . . practically I was in the hospital of the boat . . . until I landed in Seattle."

Bibiana came to finish her education but got married instead. Within eight years she would be a widow with five young children to support during the Depression. However, in 1928, when given the opportunity to come to America, future hardships were the furthest thoughts from her mind.

There were three hundred Filipinos on the boat but she was the only woman among them. When the ship's officers found out she was the only *Pinay*, they put her in a separate room with Chinese women. But since she was seasick, she spent most of the trip in the ship's infirmary. When she arrived in Seattle, nobody came to meet her and her brother. Bibiana and James had neglected to notify their other brother and their uncle as to when they were arriving. They hailed a taxi and asked the driver to take them to a place where they could stay until their relatives picked them up.

"And the taxi driver said, 'Oh, I know the place where Filipinos usually go. . . . He drove us to Chinatown. I didn't know what Chinatown is and I didn't know if that's the proper place we should go, but he thought that was the place Filipinos . . . go. We asked him, 'Is there any hotels we can go to?' . . . So we went to the Chinese hotel and boy, did I have such an unhappy time at that place . . . even though I just came from the Philippines, I never lived like that . . . I started crying.

Their hotel room had a bed, stove and sink. They went downstairs and found a grocery store. While purchasing food, they were seen by a Filipino who knew their uncle, Paul Bigornia, who then was sent for. Paul moved them to a Filipino boarding house operated by Valeriano Laigo.

Although Bibiana had intended to continue her studies, she did not enroll in school immediately, but occupied herself with housekeeping duties at the boarding house. Her uncle was nervous leaving her alone with so many men while he and the two brothers were working. He decided the family would move. Her uncle also decided she had two options: to get married or be sent back to the Philippines. Bibiana was upset because she had planned to go to school in America; she also was not interested in marrying anyone. However, her uncle had already selected a husband for her — Valeriano Laigo, who owned the boarding house where she had been staying.

Valeriano was quiet and shy, and he and Bibiana rarely spoke to one another. Valeriano had approached her uncle for permission to propose to her. Her uncle was pleased since he was just the type of person he wished his niece to marry. Her uncle said it would not look right if Valeriano proposed whlie she was living in his boarding house. Therefore, the family had to move to a hotel.

When Valeriano finally proposed, Bibiana told him she still intended to go to school and did not want to disappoint her mother. He informed her he would send her to school if she desired. Valeriano was a contractor who also owned several small businesses. He had come to America when he was barely eighteen years old in 1918. He was well respected in the small Filipino community and had brought over and provided for a number of young relatives from the Philippines.

After they received approval from her parents in the Philippines, Bibiana and Valeriano were married in 1928. Their oldest son was born on a later vacation trip to the Philippines. The family grew quickly — first a daughter and then two more sons joined the family, as well as the countless relatives who also came to live with them.

The Laigo family rented a home in the Central Area of Seattle.

"I was tired of renting, so we decided to buy. And lucky thing he was able to buy even though none of the other Filipinos were able to buy houses. Yet, in those days we had a friend who was a real estate man, who sold us this house."

Bibiana was pregnant with their fifth child when Valeriano was shot and killed in 1936 by a mentally unbalanced business acquaintance. Bibiana suddenly was faced with the responsibility of raising her young children alone.

She also had to contract her husband's cannery workers, run his cannery business, handle his books, buy supplies and tend to his (now her) cannery workers' needs. Most of the workers were her husband's relatives and provincemates. But in those days the unions were becoming strong, and they were giving her trouble over her only source of livelihood, which was contracting cannery workers.

"It was not my fault my husband died. But my children have to eat and so do I. This is the only kind of job I know I can do for the present in my pregnant condition . . . and whenever I send the boys to Alaska, because not all the boys were union members, so they (union) boycott me. But I'd send my boys to Alaska. Two policemen carrying guns would always guard me — side by side, because you know this union, with those big clubs in their hands, they block the gate to the boat."

The combined stress of running the cannery business, one of her son's health problems, and the court trial of her husband's murderer caused Bibiana to lose weight. To top it off she was also operating a restaurant to try to make ends meet.

"I get up at six in the morning, then I bring my children with me over there (the restaurant). Keep them apart in room in back. Come home at eight in the evening. Wash clothes, iron the clothes . . . fixing the papers, budget and everything, so the time I go to sleep is two o'clock. Then I get up at six in the morning because I have to help the children . . . prepare the food and everything. We had some help. A sixteen-year-old girl who used to take care of them (the children) in the house some of the time while I go and work."

Bibiana's friends and business associates encouraged her to quit working so hard, but she had five children to support, not an easy task during the Depression.

Her parish priest suggested she consider marrying again. She had had a number of suitors, and in 1938 she married Mike Castillano, a former chauffeur who was working for the Jesuits at Seattle College (later Seattle University). Four more children — a son and three daughters — blessed this marriage. And her new husband raised her other older children as his own.

In order to help her husband with food, clothing and parochial school tuition expenses, Bibiana worked on as a seamstress while the children were young. She sewed theatrical costumes during the late '30s and clothing and sleeping bags for the U.S. Army during World War II. She also designed embroidery transfers for a wholesaler.

Bibiana has been very active in the Filipino community — teaching children Philippine folk dances and sewing costumes for various programs.

In her mid-60s she began painting; some of her work has been exhibited and she has won a few awards. Today Bibiana and Mike — a retired cook — are constantly surrounded by children, grandchildren and great-grandchildren.

Belen Guzman Braganza

"My uncle decided that he would send one of his relations to school over here. I had two cousins competing with me, see, and I won it. My uncle had a sister, that's my mother, and a brother had three children, but the girl was too young to compete . . . anyway, I sort of beat them. I was really glad because I really wanted to go to school, and it was hard for my mother to put us through . . . because my father died."

Maria Belen Guzman was the only female among two hundred Filipino students attending the University of Washington during the early 1930s. She came to the United States when she was sixteen. Born in Manila, she was the second of four children. Her father, an architect, had died when she was seven. He left his family some houses and a small store, but her mother supported her children by selling jewelry. Belen stayed with her grandmother and helped in her restaurant.

Belen's uncle had enlisted in the U.S. Army in 1903. When Belen was selected to study in America, her uncle financed her trip. Since she was underage, Belen traveled with a chaperone, Alpina Zamora, a school teacher. Their trip from Manila to Seattle via Hong Kong, Shanghai and Yokohama took twenty-one days.

> "I arrived in Seattle, September 6, 1930. And at that time, the Port of Seattle was Smith Cove, which is Pier 91 now. And as I arrived, from . . . the waterfront . . . from Pike or even beyond Pike, clear down to almost Holgate, those are all lean-tos and shacks and terrible things because it was Depression. They called it Hooverville. So, I turn to my uncle and said, 'Is this America? This is terrible' . . . This was my first impression."

Belen had no problems going through immigration. (Filipinos were not "aliens" then but "nationals." The Philippines at that time was a territory of the United States — similar to Puerto Rico and Guam.) She lived in the University District home owned by her uncle, who had retired from the Navy. Although he was not a citizen, his many years of active service in the Navy entitled him to own property, a right denied other Filipino nationals.

> "It was an eight-room house. I had a real bedroom for myself. He had it . . . furnished real nice. He was a bachelor and I was really impressed. Those Filipinos over here now . . . knew my uncle . . . he was a draftsman at the navy yard."

Belen attended Broadway High School and graduated in 1932.

> "Then I attended the University of Washington until 1934. And when Seattle College (later Seattle University) opened its doors to women, I attended the first coed class and took my theology, philosophy and psychology. Seattle College was the college part of Seattle Preparatory. . . . Father McGoldrick was president at that time . . . . There were two of us (Filipina women) at Seattle University — Miss Zamora and there were about, I would say, four or five Filipinos. Then I went

back to the University of Washington and finished in the school of home economics."

Her former chaperone was the house mother for several single young men from Belen's home province of Pangasinan in the Philippines. One of these men was Belen's future husband, Bonafacio Braganza, a 1932 graduate of Washington State College in Pullman. Her uncle, who came from the Tagalog province in the Philippines, did not approve her dating young men from other regions of the Philippines.

"The Ilocanos won't mix with the Visayans. The Visayans won't mix with Ilocanos and the Tagalogs are the worst. When I was dating my husband, (my uncle) said, 'Why do you want to go with him, he's just an Ilocano?' and I said, 'He's Pangasinan.' 'They're all the same to me,' he said."

Their courtship began in 1933 and continued for five years. In the meantime she also attended University Secretarial School and learned typing skills, which enabled her to earn money to send her youngest brother and sister in the Philippines to school. In 1938 she graduated from the University of Washington and soon after married Bonifacio Braganza. Jobs were scarce, so Belen settled down to be a housewife. She taught at Maryknoll School as a volunteer.

She was active in community and church activities and was an original member of the Filipino Women's Club.

The club continued until World War II. During the war, Belen and Mrs. Luvi DeCano founded the Philippine Red Cross. They sewed, knitted, made pajamas, hospital slippers and night watch caps for the service men. They also took survival courses.

"We had a hard time . . . practically had to beg to get our thread to sew with . . . Luvi and I used to go to Chinatown and knock at the doors of the (Filipino) gambling joints there and begged for a few dollars to buy the thread we use, because the Red Cross supplies us all the bolts of materials, but our share was, you know, at least the thread."

After the war, new immigrants — especially women — came to Seattle. The Filipino community was growing with families and new organizations formed. By this time Belen had two children and she was involved in their school activities.

"I was raising my family and I was also teaching part time . . . I was made athletic director for St. Teresa (parish) and I did not accept any pay . . . I just go there usually about half hour before school ends and then work there about two or three hours . . . go to the games. I was a coach for the girls—basketball, softball, volleyball, track. We even won the all-city trophy."

With her children in Catholic school and approaching high school Belen began to plan for college expenses. She knew her husband's civil service job would not be able to accommodate increasing college costs at the Catholic university where she wanted to send her children. She began to look for a job and discovered that a teaching position at a parochial school would only pay $240 a month.

"I said, 'I got to get a job that will pay.' So I got a job in the waterfront. I worked as a cannery worker first . . . that didn't pay enough . . . so I went into 'cold storage' which paid a little more. I joined the Teamsters and it helped a great deal to help support my children through school . . . my children worked hard . . . during the summer. . . . I just kept on until I was ready to retire."

Her two children graduated from Seattle University; her daughter is now an artist, her son a physicist. Belen remains active today in the Marian Club, a Catholic senior citizen organization.

Cecilia Concepción Alvarez

Las Quatas
(oil painting)

My art work deals with concepts of feminism and culture as seen in humanistic dialogs and expressions. I like to explore female existence, validating woman's personal experience, as well as exemplifying unacknowledged female social and political contributions. My most recent series of paintings deals with the concepts of woman's social/cultural power and political sacrifice. I like to use strong colors and rich imagery to celebrate the ancient as well as contemporary dignity of womankind.

El Eterno Sueño del Danzón de la Unidad
(oil painting)

Mujer
(wood block print)

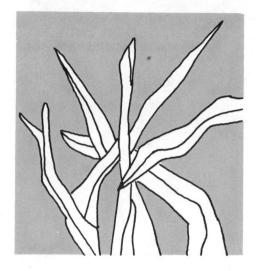

In Order to Survive

"In Order to Survive"

Introduction

Few people go around these days asking what "white culture" is. But for those of us who would never be asked that question, we may have been asked: What is Black culture? What is Indian culture? What is Hispanic culture? What is Asian culture? And once asked, we are supposed to have an answer.

Sometimes the question means: What's it like to be Black? What's it like to be Indian? What's it like to be Hispanic or Asian? And once asked, we are supposed to have an answer. Does anyone ask, what's it like to be white? Perhaps the question went out of fashion with the phrase, "Free, white and 21." Did any of us ever say, "Yes, I'm free, Black and 21!"

For those of us who have spent most of our lives in this country and can be identified as ethnic people of color, the question of one's cultural awareness is a problem. Surely it is more than one's being the victim of exploitation and racism. Surely it is more than mom, apple pie, baseball, soul food, the Fourth of July, afros and bembe dresses, Martin Luther King Day.

What else then?

Culture presupposes ties or that which people hold in common. Within the group there is agreement about values, goals, aesthetics. In the late 1960s, for example, Addison Gayle, Jr., edited an anthology called *The Black Aesthetic*. The book represented those artists and writers who believed in a political stance — Black nationalism and an artistic stance which supported the politics: the two were inseparable. There was no agreement among Black Americans, at that time, about the validity of that book — nor is there agreement now, some twenty years later. One can still ask, what is Black culture and get a range of answers. Witness, for example, the debate on college campuses about the courses called *Black Studies* or *Afro-American Studies.* Some campuses have a Black Student Union, others have a Pan African Union.

Awareness presupposes that we have a notion of something particular — let's say of oneself. Awareness also presupposes itself as a starting point. Let's say familiarity or recognition is the next step. Or definition. Thus the question becomes one of how aware we are of ourselves in our own eyes, rather than through the eyes of others. How can we recognize ourselves? How can we define ourselves in terms of our cultural experiences, in terms of our being women of color?

Let me give you two examples of my own cultural awareness. Once upon a time I taught Black literature courses at the University of Washington here in Seattle. I used a text called *Black Voices.* In it I found an essay by George E. Kent, "Ethnic Impact in American Literature (Reflections on a Course)." Kent describes one of the earliest ethnic courses, his own, to be given in a predominantly white university (Wesleyan University, Connecticut). He begins this way:

> When we speak of Negro cultural values, we encounter certain liberals and some Negroes who are wont to say that what we are talking about is habits deriving from slavery and the ghettoes — and let's get rid of them wholesale. Their attitude accepts unconditionally those unrelieved sociological images of the maimed and the diseased and the perverted. The images are powerful because, like frozen food in the supermarkets, they package easily, market easily, and are arranged easily on the shelves of the compartments of our minds; but they seem to me to be insufficiently related to the density and complexity of reality. (p. 691)

Kent goes on to list ten characteristics or key values that he found reflected in Negro folk literature and outstanding Negro writers. Three of them include: (1) "Humor as a tool for transcendence;" (2) "A sense of something more than this world and of its rhythms;" (3) "Ceremonies of poise in a non-rational universe."

Amazing, thought I to myself. Had I really been looking at myself and at Black writers with the eyes of others? Yes, I had. But could I do anything about it? Then, one day one of my students said in class, "One person's stereotype is another person's archetype." Brilliant, thought I to myself. Why hadn't I the vision or the wit to say it first?

Then came a whole raft of sisters who turned me around with their vision and mother wit. To name a few: Gwendolyn Brooks, Christine Hunter, Margaret Walker, Toni Morrison, June Jordan. As Alice Walker puts it, our mothers and their mothers have led legions of headragged generals without knowing what they were about. Because of our mothers, our women writers, we got over. I got over.

Now it's 1984, the year of Orwellian prophecies. But I'm not thinking of this awesome year as much as I am of 1863. For some reason I thought of some hypothetical novel that could have been set 120 years back, give or take a year either way. And that's when it hit me. All Black people in this country are only four generations away from slavery . . .

There's an African proverb that says, "Remember, hippopotamus, as you go upstream, your home is at the mouth of the river." As women of color, we are constantly moving up and down the river which has many names. If we know we're on a river that has a name, we have some awareness. If we know where the mouth of this river is and we can name it, we have a sense of culture. Thus the concept of cultural awareness is an imperative for us as editors of *Gathering Ground.*

As people of color we live in at least two worlds — the larger world of the country itself, and the smaller world defined by color. Yet within that smaller world, there may .be other divisions, other factions. And for us as women of color, there are worlds within these worlds. One can ask what is the culture of women of color? We believe the selections in this section present some of the range of answers. Each writer is aware of the differences that define her world(s). Each writer has a sense of her own river(s).

'Nuff said!

J. T. Stewart

Yvonne Yarbro-Bejarano

In Order to Survive

guns & butter/that's all you hear about these days/and every day there's less butter to go around/and more guns/bigger and better guns/the war on poverty is now the war on the poor/certain breeds grow strong/in the climate of war hysteria/the KKK is bolder now/the new clucks burn their crosses farther north/and ride the border with the migra/Moral Majority/the new Mafia wave their hit lists of senators and sex films and sing/"God, guts and guns/made this country what it is today"/the Right-to-Lifers chant/while the Lifers-with-no-Rights bleed/in every prison across the nation/ "O say can you see/by the dawn's early blast"/and the cowboy cult feeds its mechanical bulls/silver buckled hats and boots/strut and flex their military muscle and croon/"Mamas don't let your cowboys grow up to be presidents"/but there's another breed/that sings a different song/the survivalists/swarm to the Northwest
to the hills of Snohomish County
to the hills of Eastern Washington
to the hills of Idaho
to the hills of Southern Oregon
where the terrain reduces the risk of nuclear fallout/the survivalists/thin, hard men in sweatshirts and Army caps/steel lined eyes glinting barrel gun grey/and tight white lips clamp down hard/ on the will to survive against all odds
to survive the terrorists
to survive the thugs
to survive the Russians
to survive the nuclear holocaust
to survive the other survivors
to survive you need guns
not your run of the mill .45 pistol/you need a Streetsweeper/a 20 round 12 gauge semi-automatic drum load shot gun/guaranteed at 50 yards/or a good bolt action rifle with a military round/to survive you need lead lined bunkers cut into hillsides/with crows nests

commanding all approaching roads/concrete shelters built underground/with independent energy systems and a year's supply of food/$800,000 survival home specials/with radiation monitoring protection equipment/and knockout gas security control/the Practical Survivalist Newsletter prints manuals on how to survive
how to barter
how to reload
how to make bullets
advertises civil defense products
medical supplies
assault rifles
knives
ammunition
sample armories for every budget

like giant slow turtles the survivalists have withdrawn/heads and limbs from the cities they judge insane/withdraw sons and daughters from the schools/to educate them at home/they say they owe it to their families/the children glow with the eerie light of the perpetually afraid/like skittish colts they roll their eyes towards the Army surplus body bags/ready in case one of them dies in the attack/and listen to their father say/"you have to get violent in order to survive"

J. T. Stewart

The White Horse Cafe

They got out of Shelley's big rented freeway killer, rolled up the windows, locked the doors, and stood on the sidewalk—the three white women laughing and talking and talking; Bruce, the Indian, not smiling and not talking; and Rebecca, the black woman, closest to the curb, remaining apart from the others. A swift July breeze, coming up from the dock, singled her out and for a long moment chilled her. She unrolled her sweater and put it around her shoulders.

Still shivering, Rebecca scanned the street to her right—the place where docks and pilings and tin sheds and water and flat landscape all came together. A full red moon hung low over the horizon looking like a gigantic bloodshot eye, the disembodied eye of a cyclops. Her shivering changed to a shudder and she wondered if the others were paying attention to her.

Of course not. Her friends were having too good a time looking forward to this new place, the White Horse Cafe, in this hick town. "Think we'll ever find some decent food?" Shelley had asked two hours after they'd pulled off the ferry—the sun going low in the west and all of them hungry, their weekend on the peninsula getting underway.

"What a nothing place this is," Liz had observed about the endless trees and unmarked roads, then, "Do you think we'll see any Indians?" And from Trudy, "Hell, no, they're all safe on reservations no where near here," and Rebecca inwardly wincing at what sounded like insensitivity, if not downright ignorance, nevertheless joined in: "Hi yo, Silver. Me Kimosabe. Me Tonto." And they'd all laughed.

That's when they'd seen him walking along the highway: stove pipe hat, long braids, head band, black frock coat, faded jeans, caramel-colored boots with pointed toes.

"Holy Jesus, a real honest-to-god live one," Shelley said, slowing down to give him the once over. "Anybody care if we pick him up?" "Not me," Liz said, "maybe I can get some points for my Anthro paper." Trudy gave a silent, nodding approval, and from Rebecca, in a low mocking voice, "Let's see if he's got some wooden nickels."

They sat him on the plush back seat between Liz and Trudy. Then: speeding along the quiet, winding roads, the radio screaming rock-a-billy music, they traded just enough information to identify themselves as dormitory friends from the state's largest college, and find out that their new passenger was indeed an Indian and was willing to go as far as they were going; and, yes, they could get something to eat in the little waterfront town about eight miles ahead — they had a choice, six taverns and the White Horse Cafe.

"You two will make quite a hit," Shelley commented referring to Bruce and Rebecca. "Hope these hicks are ready for genuine ethnics." And Rebecca had laughed with her friends. "I'm ready for all . . . all comers," she added. She almost said rednecks, but not wanting to hurt her friends had backed off.

Only once had the Indian said anything to the black woman. "Got a cigarette?" he asked tapping Rebecca on her shoulder. And when she turned around, pack extended over the seat, she read the questions in his eyes. *What are you doing here? Why are you playing betrayal games?* And she tossed the cigarettes into his lap without speaking.

From the open car window, the warm July air heating her flushed face, Rebecca saw neither the cows moving slowly on a hillside or the squat box-shaped Grange Hall. Instead, she focused on her own uneasiness. Who was he to make her worry about what she'd said? Or her friends. After all, she'd stopped straightening her hair. Wasn't that enough to insure her identity?

And now they were standing outside the White Horse Cafe in three distinct groups: Shelley, Liz and Trudy, in jeans and tank tops, laughing and talking; Bruce, tall and silent, off to one side, looking like a bronze Abe Lincoln with turquoise rings and bracelets; and Rebecca at the curb, staring out toward the water, shivering in her African style dress, her sweater over her shoulders.

Why was she so cold?

The White Horse Cafe. Back there on the road it had seemed like a terrific idea to come here. Food — maybe a pizza and a few drinks. At any moment they'd have to go in.

Rebecca closed her eyes and rocked back and forth. How could she tell these liberated women, her white friends, how she felt at times about going to a new place. Back home, in the city or on campus, she was o.k. She knew where to go, how to act. She could disappear in its bigness and not have to worry. She could dress the way she wanted to, style her hair the way she wanted to — an afro, cornrows. And usually some other black person, perhaps a complete stranger, would tell her how good she looked. But out here on this strange street with the red-eyed moon hanging low over the water, she felt cold and alone.

And what about Bruce, the Indian? Where did he get off calling her a bigot?

Then the command came to move into enemy territory. "Come on, slow poke," Shelley called. "Get your feet in gear."

Rebecca took three deep breaths, looked up and down the wide street with its unlit, dark anonymous stores or ships and its assortment of pickups and two-toned cars front-angle parked along the high curb like slanted dominoes, their unwinking eyes monitoring the five trespassers. Or so she thought. Then she saw Shelley, leading the way as usual, across the street to a flat grey building with blue-white neon lettering, the others following, and she reminded herself that this little waterfront town was only picturesque and historical. Nothing else. Nothing else.

Rebecca followed the others into the air-conditioned, fluorescent lit White Horse Cafe. The screen door banged shut behind her. She felt her eyes and skin react to the harsh lights and freezing air. And to something even deeper.

Bang.

They were all there, fresh from the nightmare she dared not dream. They were sitting at booths by the long window. They were sitting on revolving stools at the high counter. They were conjured up from some old movie, the violent kind she always avoided. They were all there, the ones she dreaded: the red moon faces with small sunken eyes; the eagle-like noses and the pointed Adam's apples; the lacquered bouffant hairdos; the sprayed shingle cuts; the blue and green crusted eye shadow; the red checkered neck scarves; the polyester pants suits — lavenders, hot pinks, lemon yellows; the small white fingers with crimson polished nails; the faded blue shirts with button down collars; the high white cowboy hats with their middles indented like valleys between snowy mountain ranges; the suntanned arms with anchor tattoos.

And: glassed-in rows of pies — apple, coconut, cream, custard, lemon meringue; carefully tiered maple bars and powdery cake doughnuts and corrugated old fashioned doughnuts; scuffed vinyl mosaic floor; beige laminated table tops and counters; the deep hum of some generator back in the kitchen, behind the swinging doors, that kept everything running.

Where were the others? *Betrayal. Betrayal.* That word kept saying itself in her head.

Where were the others? Now Rebecca could see Shelley leading the other women *(women?—weren't they her friends?)* through a side alcove marked Dining Room. Bruce, the Indian—now she thought of him only as the Indian—stood less than two feet away in the aisle between the booths and the counter. She realized: that he was waiting for her; that she was standing in the center of an eating area, obviously a cafeteria.

That almost everyone was drinking something: beer in tall schooners, coffee in thick white mugs, iced tea in frosted glasses, soft drinks in bottles. Over their drinks, they were looking at her. And at the Indian. She read their eyes and their eyes paralyzed her.

Fear. Meanness.

Here it was again. Fear bordering on meanness in its raw, unspoken form. How could the women *(her friends?)* understand what she was reading in the eyes of these strangers, those who *(for the moment?)* were too polite, too civilized to voice their anger and rage about her presence among them. "When you get scared, you get mean," someone had said to her once.

But it was the Indian, too. They were afraid of him as well. Centuries of guilt—real and imagined—with no place to go. Except at them. She and the Indian were in the center of a wheel, its spokes radiating out to the observers in the White Horse Cafe. He in braids and turquoise and she in African Bembe dress and large afro held their attention. Still she read their eyes.

Their eyes said: *It is after sundown. This is our town. Never mind phrases like "Red Power" or "Black is Beautiful." Never mind symbols of pride like braids and afros. Here dark skins and ethnic pride are non-negotiable.*

Here in the White Horse Cafe the old scenarios, the old myths that lived at the edge of everyone's eye could be reactivated at any moment.

Was this the moment?

From the center of the wheel, Rebecca heard the Indian think her name; an unvoiced part of her responded as she stared at him. He in his soundless Shaman way was calling her out; he quickstepping to her side; he pushing her by her elbow; he neutralizing her demon view; he propelling her toward the side alcove marked Dining Room. As she moved like one dispossessed of will, like one stripped of mind, she knew a compassionate spirit had taken her from that circle of darkness, of terror; that somewhere and somehow she had met him before.

She thought of an Indian great-grandmother she'd heard about once that she could never trace. And in Bruce's touch *(yes, Bruce again)*, she'd felt resemblances: an owl's wing, blue moccasins, sunflower seeds.

But now they were in the darkened alcove of the dining room. Behind them, as though by prearranged signal, conversations started, dishes and silverware clinked together, and the jukebox blared itself into life — in the lyrics, something about a down and out lover from El Paso. The nightmare had backed away. And she was safe.

Jo Cochran

For Paula

We are closer than blood, in the midnight
          the vision is clear,
we are talking our lives, power runs between
us. No longer afraid, I tell you, I hungered
          for you, before I knew
what was needed. Talking like this of ourselves,
          north, south, east, west,
our people are hidden for survival, growing
in windbreaks, or places barren of soil.
          We are talking our lives,
to the corners of the universe, to comfort each other
as Mother to daughter.

Reading Shadow Country by Paula Gunn Allen

When I read your poems, inside
I am truly breathing. Breathing
with the air between mesas, then the dry
sweet soil, as we ride what is more than wind,
what is time and life. Is this how
we could have always talked to each other?
Without hesitations, but in an always,
all ways, speech of body, heart and mind
in unison, in deep song.

I am worn, but there must be singing,
recountings, blankets and bean pots.
There must be a keeping of the spirits,
Changing Woman, dukwibu7, Basket Ogress, Thought Woman,
our selves, our people are in transition
between earth and sky, that not so long ago was one.

I think of my people here, in the long ago
getting together to push the sky up with poles,
because too many people kept getting lost,
jumping off into the sky because it was too close
to the ground. Sometimes, those who jumped
would find a way back, or become stars in the night,
or get caught in the inbetween, the horizon.

When, I think I am worn, like now,
I think after that horizon, and being not quite ready
to do my singing. But, now I have slept
a night wrapped in your blanket, the one woven
with the colors of the setting sun,
I have read your poems, and you are singing,
my elders are singing and we are still
pushing up the sky.

Doris Harris

Who Will Braid My Hair Today?

Even though I'm an adult Black woman and I'm out on my own, supposedly able to deal with life, I've always had my grandmother braid my hair before or after every big decision. Like when I recited "The Woodpecker's Song" in the first grade, when I got my first pair of heels, or when I started my "woman's thing" and thought I was bleeding to death. She was always there. She would sit me down on my pillow on the floor between her big warm thighs that smelled the way grown ladies are supposed to smell. She would brush my hair until it glistened, using her big brown hands with the zillion callouses from "the fields of life." So strong and gentle, I always wanted to grab them and kiss the palms; I never did. She would brush and talk and braid and sing.

When her friends would gather as they always did and speak of the past — about how much cotton they used to pick down South and how glad they were to be up North and free — my grandmother would laugh. With her head thrown back, her breasts would bounce and her laugh would make me laugh even though I wasn't really sure what I was laughing at.

The comb would become a conductor's baton. And when she had everyone's attention, she would say, "Fool, you're still in the field, only you just can't see it. When you've got to go to the Welfare Office, you're still picking. When you're sitting there waiting for them to call your number, you're still picking . . . picking which story to tell that pasty-faced social worker about the father of your kids. Picking which dance you'll have to dance to explain the new t.v. set you got from hitting the numbers. Pick, Nigger, pick!" Her laugh would become bitter and through the "Amens" and "Yes, Lawds" of her friends, I would tug at her through her house dress and say, "Brush, Grandma, brush."

She would braid my hair fast or slow, depending on how pleased or cross she was with me. I would bring out all my good-graded papers, no matter how old. I would recite "The Lord's

Prayer," do my times tables all the way to ten before each braiding and just listen to her advice: on men and women, women and women, women and the world. Death. She knew everything.

Who will braid my hair now?

She was there when I was sixteen. That was a fast braiding day, the way all the days then seemed to be. "I'm pregnant," I blurted out. It either was the tightness of the braids or the hopelessness I felt inside that made me confess.

"What you want to do, Girl?" she asked, not missing a strand.

"I don't want to be a mother. I want more," I said louder than necessary.

"There's some who say you've got all a woman needs."

"But I'm not a woman." I began to stammer, "I need to be . . . I want more, Grandma." I cried low and long on her big warm thighs that smelled the way a grown woman is supposed to smell.

"We'll take care of this, and we never need to think on this again," she said.

Through high school and college, heartbreaks, failures and successes, she's been there. My friends at college would laugh at me for running home every chance I got, to see my grandmother and get my hair braided. Those same sisters were paying some stranger to do their hair but not getting any advice — not even getting favorite recipes like hot water cornbread or yam pie.

Today, they put my grandmother's hands to rest, folded in such an unnatural way: no comb, no brush, no love. The church elders thought me cold and unfeeling as they tried to lead me away. I kept asking and asking, "Who will braid my hair . . . who will braid my hair today?"

Vickie Sears

Sticktalk

I was walking alone through a coastal village feeling lonely and pensive. Glad to be on a reservation. That in itself made it safer for many feelings and perhaps riddle answers to recent puzzlings. I was thinking about going to the Shaker ceremony in the morning. It had been a long time since I had participated in any ceremonies other than pow-wows. I'd been living in the city for almost three years. A concrete-caught citizen far away from the smell of sweat lodges with water-splashed spitting rocks. Missed the sounds and smells of old ways ceremonies.

It seemed especially important at this time because I had been reminiscing about drinking for weeks. There was struggle staying sober. I'd been sober for eleven years. Even recently celebrated that anniversary but the wall of protection seemed fragile. Almost every recent day my mind tongue tasted the bitter heat of scotch. I salivated. It seemed real again. That getting drunk would make everything better. All the world issues and ordinary life problems would fade to oblivion. Nothing would hurt. I would have control of my environment again. Fools talk on a fools walk. Splurges of dirges, I mused. .

I passed broken window houses. Abandoned trailers. Homes with woodpiles and bicycles in the yards. Odd piles of beer cans and bottles. I didn't want to think about what the rate of alcoholism might be in the village. Didn't want to be reminded of a major disease of my people. Or myself. Those were social worker's thoughts. Images of internalized oppression and all. I was supposed to be resting. Began to cry, when I heard an Elder voice on the wind.

"Come down to the beach. Come past the lighthouse along my long beach. We'll meet."

I probably dreamed it but decided to see the lighthouse. Walked past the Tribal buildings which were Saturday empty. Skirted over logs around the lighthouse. Heard waterwaves rub rocks over each other. Saw children running in the foam in summersun on the winter's day. Smelled clams and kelp cooking. Stared at the giant out-cropped rocks before turning south on the beach. The tide was full and curling across the sand. Up and down I traversed logs, tires and heaps of floating kelp. It was cold. Clear.

The beach at this village has spirits all about. I felt them in windbrushes of ancient songs. The night before had been filled with fires, drums and dancing. I had seen the dead ones in circles of dance. Could feel them all around me now. I walked slowly, feeling their power. Wondered if I had been a coastal native in some past life or if those of other worlds just spoke to all people of all tribes. In that thought, a stick rose up to speak. It was red, brown and yellow. It was almost four feet long and waving itself in front of me. I stopped, both fearful and not.

"*Squadelich?*" I asked. "Medicine stick?"

It didn't speak. It fell, quite flat, into the sand. I walked closer. Didn't touch it. Bent down to examine it more thoroughly.

"I called you to come. You did that well, but you didn't recognize me," came an indignant response.

With that, I sat on the nearest log and waited. The stick was quiet for a time. I looked toward the sea. I didn't find it strange to be waiting on stickspeaking. My father had repeatedly proven when I was very young that all things have their own spirits and lessons to share. I am just as the sticks and rocks. I may not always know my purpose, but it will be clear to me when I need to know. I will behave just as I am supposed to at that moment. Rocks had taught me before. Children. Adults. Animals. The burning of sweet grass. Many things. So I logsat, cold in winterwind waiting for this stick to speak.

Stick began to hum. The song seemed familiar. I rocked. After a time, the stick raised itself on a jagged leg. Rested on its side.

"Peaceful here, aay?"

"Yes, stick."

"Feels good, aay?"

"Yes, stick."

"Not like the other place where you live?"

"No, stick."

"You cannot just run to hide here forever."

"True, stick."

"What do you want here?"

"I don't know. I feel confused. Can't find direction for a lot of things."

"If you return to swallowing you will lose all of you."

I didn't respond. I knew what that Elder was talking about, but hadn't completely given up thoughts of drinking. Didn't look at the stick.

It flippped off its leg and rolled toward the surf across the flat beach.

"If you don't follow you'll never have the answer!" it yelled.

My mind said, "The hell with you, stick. You're just a fantasy anyway. I'm not going to rescue you. I do enough caretaking in my work. Go away."

The stick rolled over and over on itself until it reached the edge of the receding tide. It stood straight up and twirled itself into the sand. Slight stroking ripples surrounded the stick but never strongly enough to dislodge it from the root it made for itself. Now it wasn't a matter of saving the stick. I could no longer view water, cliffs or seagullsailing without that stick being in the periphery of my vision.

Damned, I moved down the beach a few feet never looking back at the stick. This was silly to be paying attention to a stick. Calling it an Elder. The conflicts of old beliefs and semi-city-rearing pushed at me. I sat down on a big log. Began to survey the new territory. Then saw it tangled in the rubble of a new batch of debris. It was grinning at me! I looked back to where I had been and the stick wasn't there.

"Not there, aay?"

"Old stick, if you are not a medicine teacher, who are you? You seem like a person of magic. I know nothing of magic."

"Medicine sticks come to those who know them. I am not medicine I am not magic. Take me home with you."

"But you live on this beach. The city can consume you. You won't be happy in the city!"

"Not all things are bad. Take me home with you."

"Stick, you're teasing me and I'm too old for your game."

The stick did not respond. I sat a while, listening. Heard nothing. Decided again I was being foolish. Began to walk up a path away from the beach. Puzzled. Perhaps I should go back to the stick. Maybe I'd forgotten how to listen. I rounded a corner and saw the stick again. The Old One was now resting against a fat log way above high tideline right next to the path. It hummed as I neared. I smiled. Sat. Listened. Finally said, "Alright, Old One. Do you still want to come home with me?"

"Yes. You need to have me come with you. We have many things to do together."

Stick marches in the doorjamb corner at the end of the hall, ready to leap out. But then, perhaps, she sees her position in the beginning of the hall as the start of a great race. I don't know. But she's an old stick with an ancient head howling up at the sky. She screams to be remembered for an ancient nature. Pokes at me with teasing, questions or statements obliquely made.

"Your work is too much," she once intoned.

"Night is for sleep," she charged.

"Ceremony is always," she warned.

Asked, "Why did you bring me here?"

"Silly stick, I saw you on the beach and you told me to do so."

"Yes. But why?"

"You tell me, stick. You're responsible for moving here to live with me. This is my home and you're the guest."

"Humph," responded the Old One.

She didn't talk again for a week. Her head remained turned into the corner.

After a week of stick's rude silence, I said, "Alright you, you are a teacher. I acknowledge that I brought you home because you challenged me on the beach. Made me think on a thing I had in mind to do and stopped it. So I give you your acknowledgement, Old Person, willingly. I won't fight you anymore. You are more than a guest. I'm sorry. I'm ready to listen."

In the hall, I stood sticktalking. Heard an order. "Sit." Watched the stick turn its face toward me.

"It is good you have always called me an Old One. It is true. I am also your forgottens, here to remind you that alone is not always lonely. I am a root once groundgrown and anchored into the earth. As are you. Always. Listen in yourself to the old parts. They are still good. There is strength in your personal ceremony. It cannot be forgotten for days or left undone. It is your power. I am also water floater. I remind you of that. Water holds up life. Adds to all growing. And, I am a maker of fire. A giver of heat come to remind you that, as I make fire of myself, so do you. You are always in and with yourself. All things are interwoven with others. Nothing can grow or live entirely alone. Enough is said. I am here. You are in you. I am in you."

The stick stopped speaking. I waited for more but there was none then. She's spoken since. I stop to listen each day now. Touch her in leaving or coming, thanking her for being a friend. Thank the Hall of Grandmothers and the Creator for gifting me sticktalk.

Sue Chin and Mayumi Tsutakawa

Mien and Hmong Women's Textile Work

Illustrations by Margaret A. Davidson

In the Northwest, we are fortunate to have a large settlement of Southeast Asian refugees of the Mien and Hmong nomadic mountain tribes of Laos. The intricate and superb indigo dyeing and needlework the women of these tribes practice is age old, but is being adapted to their new home in America.

This fine craft work, which is best shown off in the women's costumes of the Mien and Hmong, is finding a place among the ethnic crafts of America. Training to help the native women run their own sales outlets and promotion of the craft work is growing.

We decided to talk with a leader among the Mien needleworkers to find out her story.

Farm Kouei Saeteun has come far since she fled the Communist takeover of Laos almost ten years ago. Resourceful, ambitious and industrious, Farm Kouei helps manage South East Asian Design Cooperative, a marketing outlet for Mien and Hmong craftswomen with a storefront in Seattle's Pike Place Market. "Farm Kouei is considered one of the leaders of the Mien women in Seattle," says Ann Thomas, president of the non-profit South East Asian Design which assists the for-profit cooperative. "A lot of the Mien women look up to her."

Farm Kouei and her family live in a small, sparsely-furnished two-story apartment in the Holly Park Housing Project in South Seattle. The young Mien tribeswoman, in a colorful traditional costume, greeted me with a shy smile when I arrived to interview her. She was alone. But by the time I left, two and a half hours later, the house had filled with family noises: her young son and his cousins, running up and down the stairs and in and out of the house; the grandmother sitting next to us bouncing the youngest family member, a seven-month-old boy, on her lap and, the telephone ringing, again and again.

The family is a very important, integral part of her life, Farm Kouei told me. She and ten members of her family, now grown to thirteen, made their way to Seattle in 1979 after spending four long and hard years in a refugee camp in Thailand. Her father and sister are still in the camp.

About 12,000 Mien and Hmong were among the Southeast Asian refugees who made Seattle their first home in the United States. Though they are preliterate tribes with no written language, they are adapting rapidly in the U.S. Many have now moved on to join relatives in other parts of the country, but a sizeable community remains and is growing in the Northwest. Some members are taking up retraining for urban service-oriented jobs, while others have found farmlands to tend in rural areas of Western Washington.

As the families' lives rapidly change, especially those of the young people, traditions such as the dyeing and needlework of the Mien and Hmong women are important as surviving evidence of the age-old traditions of costume, craft work and even storytelling.

This Hmong animal design is typical of the embroidery pieces used to tell stories of the Hmong mountain tribes, events which occurred both before and after the invasion of Laos which disrupted the nomadic but peaceful tribal existence.

As with other nomadic tribes throughout the world, the creation of costumes for the Mien and Hmong evolved as a practical and portable art form and has been practiced solely by women. New designs are constantly developed. The costumes of a tribe may be based on identifying colors used in the dyeing, embroidery or appliqué, such as with the Blue Hmong, White Hmong, Stripe Hmong. Some large Hmong embroidery pieces were created to recall a peaceful life before war, the bombs of invaders and the flight by foot from Laos to Thailand.

The Mien women's costume is based on a red-ruffed black coat with the front tucked into a wide embroidered sash. The coat is open in front to show off thoroughly embroidered culotte-like pants. The costume is worn with an embroidered turban. Men's costumes (Mien and Hmong) are simple black tops and pants. Babies are protected from evil spirits by black caps adorned with large red pompoms and silver buttons. Small children are dressed like their parents.

The intricate cross stitch of Mien embroidery may include symbols and motifs recalling legends, journeys and beliefs — or even a report of what the past year has been like.

The Mien's ancient tradition of needlework includes patterns developed from tiny cross stitches. A pair of black women's trousers might be thickly encrusted with yellow, green, red and pink embroidery. The long, wide sash and turban worn by women are similarly embroidered.

The Hmong costume is based on a short, many-pleated skirt worn over leggings and with an apron panel over it. The skirt traditionally is made from off-white, hand-woven cotton. The cotton is indigo-batiked in tiny, freehand but geometric, patterns. It is then appliquéd and embroidered as well. The process might take one month to complete. A long sash wound around the waist and a turban also are worn. Often jackets and other pieces feature appliqué on the intricate reverse appliquéd technique in which the cloth is cut and sewn back in painstaking patterns to reveal colors in the fabric underneath.

Appliqué is used by the Hmong needleworkers to create intricate geometric designs. Tiny dots (like French knots) are among the stitches added to the appliqué areas, enhancing the composition or symbolism.

For both the Hmong and Mien, new clothing is prepared for the all-important New Year's celebration, when one's best costume and silver jewelry is worn. The Southeast Asian women seem to be preserving the custom of creating and wearing these costumes, while the men and older children are rapidly rejecting the traditional costumes for more Americanized dress. Perhaps it is the pride in one's skills — and the potential for earning some money from the tradition — that causes the textile arts to persist among the women.

The cooperative sells both Hmong and Mien items. The co-op members have been marketing hand-crafted products since May 1980. Initially the needlecrafts were marketed at museums and fairs throughout Western Washington. That was how Farm Kouei got involved. "My (English as a Second Language) teacher helped me to sell my things at the fair," she said.

As a co-op manager, Farm Kouei works twenty hours a week and earns about $400 a month. "A job is important," Farm Kouei says. "If we don't have a job, we cannot earn money. We cannot take care of the whole family." With her job, Farm Kouei is able to help her husband, Yao Liam, who works at an electronic assembly plant, and his brother to support the rest of the thirteen-member extended family. Although Yao Liam says he sometimes tells Farm Kouei to spend some money on herself, Farm Kouei usually spends the money on her family.

Farm Kouei says another reason she is working at the cooperative is "because I want to help a lot of Mien women because many of my people don't have jobs."

Most of the women who volunteer at South East Asian Design Cooperative are Mien. About twenty-six Mien and six Hmong are active members. An additional fifty women have been involved in an "on call" basis. The craftswomen market cooperatively and pool their productive efforts, thereby increasing the cost-effectiveness of their efforts.

The products sold at the co-op can be divided into two categories, those made according to traditional ethnic patterns and functions, and those adapted to the American consumer. New product lines requiring a minimum of handwork and subdued colors have become popular and include personal accessories and home decorations such as wall hangings, placemats and pillows.

Farm Kouei will continue to work at the cooperative until April 1984, when the grant money that pays her salary runs out. She is hopeful that there will be money from other grants to keep her on.

What is the future of Mien and Hmong women's needlecrafts in the Northwest? It is possible the techniques and designs may change in order to please American customers and speed up production. This emphasizes the fragility of the first generation of Laotian mountain people's traditions, and the need to preserve them.

Carletta Wilson

dreamdream daybreak

dream: 1979

sitting outside
me and this girl
i call her Mel
but her name is
something else
it's dark
real dark
we sit and discuss things
i look up
see 12 moons coming
i ask
can you see them
she half-heartedly
only sees 4
i ask the guy
then count

the moons
form a line
lights of the city
red yellow little lights
glitter between them
then we feel the sting
like rain
getting thicker as we run
we run
back to the house
i wonder where to go
blow the flame
see the fluorescent falling

dream: 1983

we are home
somebody looking
how skinny my arms
they've always been this way
i say

in the front bedroom
so light
so light
it comes
and twirls twirls
right out the window
circling all the time
breaking the windows
glass rains
up/down the street
sound is high
s p l a/stic
one/right/move
will/break
the house
like toys we'll crumble

i run
to my poppa
on the porch
·in peach and pale
a face
i've never known
fear horror
skulking about
the shirt/the house/our history
i feel the sound
the breaking

daybreak

my breath
slides
smoothly off the bed
across the carpet
where questions
leap
fragment and filament

when it is spring
which bud will burst?
which colors rise?
which open/unadorned
streets will tremble
to spectacles of warmth?

in seconds grown wide
with milk and future
my body strikes dawn
with visions:
mingling/dead/matri-patriarchal/ones
monkey/rat/peacock/stranger
in restless twirl
in universe
say
"the earth
(that buxom woman)
the trees/her sons
the rivers/her daughters
the moon the sun
the life we haven't lived"
say they
in universe
"the swarming winds
the bilious seasons
the unkept, wandering hoards of us"
say we
in universe
"wake!
america wake!
america wake!
jump!your!stark!sleep!"

i wake
stride into a world
where children
those transitory beings
find their cradles
rocked by blood

these years are
strangers
quarrels
and
sudden breaks in silence

saga with mary queen of the earth

ride the rock hard, daughter
beautifully moon shines on raw flesh
breathe
wade deeply
the stones and dust
we are forever
are endless volcanic sisters of the soil
ride the rock hard, daughter
fresh red ruby tears
are kissing
are kissing us
breathe
hold him close
his name is Winter
he comes (as all males)
in seasons
what a night to behold
a thousand sparks
a lip of moon
red ruby us
specked so brown
like the flag, daughter

american and bright
against tattered skin
so brown
what a sight night beholds
ride the rock hard, daughter
til what bites
is not teeth but bone
til what gives is not breath but the soul
singing its last
humming its first
ride the rock
break the moon
ride the rock
chew the sun
ride the rock
swallow the sea
ride the rock
we are red
ride the rock
we are stained
ride the rock
we are blood
ride the rock
we are semi-precious earth
taking night into its pores
breathe
breathe deeply, stones and dust
that which you feel
that breaking apart
the crust/hungry song
is only the gristle of one life
boning into another

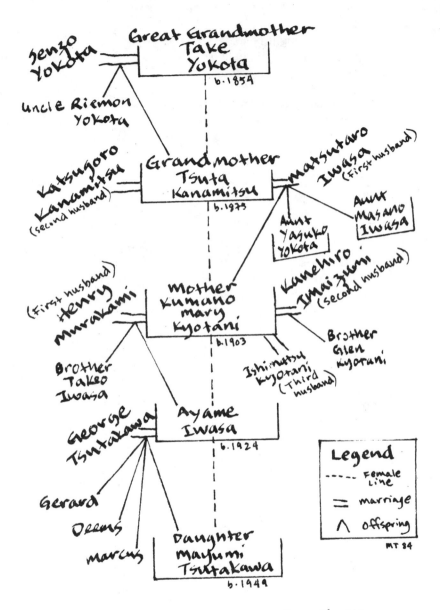

Senzo Yokota == Great Grandmother Take Yokota b.1854

Uncle Riemon Yokota

Katsugoro Kanamitsu (second husband) == Grandmother Tsuta Kanamitsu b.1873 == Matsutaro Iwasa (First husband)

Aunt Yasuko Yokota

Aunt Masano Iwasa

(First husband) Henry Murakami == Mother Kumano Mary Kyotani b.1903 == Kanehiro Imaizumi (second husband)

Brother Takeo Iwasa

Ishimatsu Kyotani (Third husband)

Brother Glen Kyotani

George Tsutakawa == Ayame Iwasa b.1924

Gerard

Deems

Marcus

Daughter Mayumi Tsutakawa b.1949

Legend
- - - - Female Line
= marriage
∧ offspring

MT 84

The Female Based Yokota Family Line

Mayumi Tsutakawa

A Chest of Kimonos —
A Female Family History

In my mother's room stands a tall pawlonia wood chest filled with kimonos. My mother's mother brought the chest from Japan and through the years filled it with the bright kimonos of my mother's childhood, the brilliant kimonos used for performing Japanese dance and the somber kimonos reserved for older people.

Each kimono has a personality and a story, as did the many women that dominated my mother's family through several generations. Their unusual stories are told in the voice of my mother, Ayame, in the following brief family history.

Interspersed with my mother's story is a historical discussion of Japanese immigration to the United States—a discussion that cries for a fuller treatment, more personal detail and more interpretation. I hope to help write that story some day.

Great-grandmother Take Yokota headed the family home on a farm near Okayama in Western Japan. Her husband, Senzo Yokata, was a Shinto priest-turned-farmer. He died in 1904; his widow lived to see many generations born in the next forty years. Take was born in 1854 during the feudal Edo period, the daughter of a samurai. The samurai class was losing importance with the coming of the modern age, but its members still kept their proud bearing and reserved manners.

Take's beautiful daughter, my grandmother Tsuta, married an adventurous young man, Matsutaro Iwasa, and had three daughters. However, after the Russo-Japanese War, in about 1907, Matsutaro sailed for America, leaving the family behind. He probably disagreed with Japan's growing militarism and perhaps had heard of the great opportunities to make money in America.

Another Yokota child, Tsuta's brother Riemon, had already left for America; the female household now consisted of Take, Tsuta and the three daughters. One of the daughters was my mother Kumano (later called Mary), a rather stocky, square-faced woman with round gold-rimmed glasses who loved to dress in the latest fashions.

At the turn of the century, Japan was desperately trying to catch up with the Western industrialized nations, partly to overcome the effects of its 250-year isolation during the feudal Edo period. In addition to initiating plans for imperialist expansion throughout Asia, the Japanese government began developing a parliamentary democracy based on a constitution, sent its scholars and students to study abroad, and adopted Western dress and culture. Isolated from these grand government schemes, the common people continued to suffer under the persistent feudal customs, which included strict obedience to the emperor-ruled government. Women suffered especially, enjoying virtually no freedoms under the Confucian-influenced patriarchal system.

The large-scale immigration of Japanese laborers to America was at first bolstered by the American decision to curtail Chinese immigration in 1882. This ended with the Gentleman's Agreement of 1907–1908, when Japan voluntarily cut off the flow of laborers, although the families of men already in the U.S. were allowed to emigrate.

The early immigrants, Issei, *bolstered by promises of good jobs and easy wealth, toiled in the face of unspeakably harsh physical and social conditions, cutting timber, blasting tunnels and fishing frozen waters. Coping with racial hatred, physical violence and work schedules stretching from before dawn to after dusk, they eventually yearned for families to relieve them of the daily hardships.*

Living in Portland, where he worked as a railroad machinist, my grandfather Matsutaro Iwasa remarried and sent for the two younger of his daughters, Kumano and Yasuko, in 1917. His oldest daughter was in high school in Kobe, so she stayed in Japan. Take and Tsuta kept the family home in Okayama. The teenage daughters suffered under their harsh stepmother. Soon after, tragedy struck when their father died of a sudden heart attack at the age of forty.

Meanwhile, the stepmother had arranged for my mother Kumano, who adopted the American name Mary, to marry Henry Murakami. I think that the stepmother just wanted to be rid of the strong-willed 18-year-old daughter Kumano. Henry adopted the Iwasa family name since that family had no male heir.

With the death of Matsutaro, the stepmother decided to return to Japan with the urn containing his cremated remains. She took the two daughters to the funeral but decided to deposit them in

Okayama and retreat to her own family home.

In Okayama, my mother Mary found herself nauseous from pregnancy and hardly up to the rough passage back across the Pacific to her husband. Her son, my brother Takeo, was born in the Yokota family home. The mother and baby did not return to Papa Henry in Portland until the baby was a year old.

But by then Henry had engaged himself in a love affair. My mother, barely out of her teen years, left Portland and set out with the baby to find her own mother, Tsuta, who had remarried Katsugoro Kanamitsu and left Japan to relocate with him in Los Angeles. Mother also had a vague idea that her uncle Riemon lived somewhere in Southern California, operating a Chinese restaurant (Riemon had married a widow with five children and eventually would cut his ties to his family.) On the long train ride south, Mother could hardly converse with anyone as her English was still limited.

The family reunited. Henry gave up his love affair to join Mary in Los Angeles and there, in Hollywood, where Henry sometimes found work gardening for movie studios, I was born. Everyone worked in the family restaurant. My mother was the most enthusiastic, throwing every penny she earned and her entire soul into the business; she seemed to relish the constant challenge. My grandmother Tsuta travelled back and forth to Japan, visiting and helping to build up the Yokota home with her precious American dollars. On one of these trips, Tsuta took my brother Takeo, a toddler of three, and I, barely thirteen months, to stay in Okayama. No doubt two young ones created much havoc in a harried restaurant family and an unhappy marriage.

Often, children born of immigrants in America, (Nisei, or second generation) were sent "home" to Japan to be cared for by relatives. The reasons varied — sometimes immigrants had no time or money to care for many children. Other times, the reason was that the children needed a "proper upbringing" not to be found in America. Some children, called Kibei, returned to the United States, but others stayed in Japan, eventually renouncing their American citizenship during World War II.

In 1924, racist lobbies in the U.S. succeeded in getting Congress to pass the Immigration Exclusion Act with the wording that the Japanese were an "unassimilable race," — meaning they could never become loyal American citizens because their heritage was too strong and their customs too strange.

Without the steady influx of immigrants to fuel the transient frontier labor force, Japanese communities came to depend on agricultural work, the service trades and their own businesses. Despite the Depression, they held on: stable, isolated communities in which the first generation immigrants (Issei) could not become U.S. citizens. Highly literate, the people of these communities supported many newspapers, cultural societies political groups.

Soon enough, Papa Henry left once again for other fortunes. Though she worked day and night, my mother chanced to meet young Imaizumi, a London-educated heir to a major construction family in Japan, who happened to travel through Los Angeles. Taken by my mother's independent spirit, he married her, despite his family's discouragement. This was probably the happiest time in my mother's life. A son, my stepbrother Glen, was born. But it all ended when Imaizumi died of an incurable illness in 1931, after only two years of marriage.

Mother took baby Glen and her husband's ashes back to the Imaizumi family home in Shizuoka. The rich Imaizumi family paid her a generous sum but did not wish to embrace an unknown daughter-in-law (who had been previously married), or her baby son, although he was of the family blood. With the money, my mother invested in a new Japanese restaurant in Los Angeles, and purchased land in Japan to support Takeo and me, her two other children still living in the Yokota family home.

After a visit with Takeo and me in Okayama, Mother returned to Los Angeles with Glen, whose grandmother Tsuta began to take care of him.

In Japan, Takeo and I lived with mother's oldest sister Masano, who had briefly been married to and widowed by a Kobe ship's captain before returning to Okayama. Takeo and I grew up together and felt we had only each other for security in a world without parents and a constantly changing set of relatives.

For a time, we lived in a duplex in a village outside Okayama, built with money sent by my mother. Despite having us to care for, Aunt Masano carried on a love affair with a married man; he came and stayed nearly every night for several years. Perhaps this is why Takeo often begged my mother to take me back to America, so that, at the innocent age of thirteen, I wouldn't be forced to live in such a household. Takeo himself felt a deep loyalty to Aunt Masano and sadness that she never had her own children. He stayed in Japan to finish high school business courses, and rather than come back to America, went to work for the Kawasaki shipbuilding factory in Osaka until he was drafted by the Japanese Imperial Army to fight in China.

Divorced and widowed, my mother worked hard, long hours at the restaurant, but contemplated a third marriage—this time to the liquor dealer Kyotani from Sacramento. Before marrying him, she came back to Japan to check on the remainder of her family and decided that I should be brought back to the United States. Her arrival in our village was the event of the year. She drove a big Oldsmobile over the rough country roads that had probably never had a car driven on them — and she wore expensive slacks in that rural place where women never wore anything but rough field clothing and straw zori sandals.

At thirteen, I was an American citizen, but knew nothing of America—I was *Kibei*—and therefore much more like the first generation *Issei* than the almost totally Americanized second generation *Nisei*. In 1937 I came back "home" to Sacramento, to an unfamiliar family and life.

Meanwhile, Japan had embarked on a full-scale imperialist course of destruction. The country had suffered unequal treaties with Western nations and was fighting to rise from its second-class position in the world. Japan intended to show the world it had the military might to gain any territories it needed. Japan annexed Taiwan and Korea in 1910, then went on to take over portions of China in the '20s and '30s.

Rural life probably proved to be the most stable existence in those turbulent times. Farmers continued to plant and harvest rice as they had for a millenium, while in urban areas, factories geared up for major military production.

In the U.S., an anti-Japanese campaign sprung up in Chinese communities as Japan began its ruthless expansion, stripping its conquered colonies of raw materials and their indigenous cultures, and requiring Japanese to be the language of instruction.

The Japanese in America watched with growing apprehension as the old feudal Japan transformed itself into a new Imperialist Japan.

With the threat of war between the two nations, Grandmother Tsuta and her husband Kanamitsu decided to leave Los Angeles and return to Japan. But when they got to Okayama, Kanamitsu opted to return to his family home instead of joining the Yokota clan.

Our household in Japan continued to be female-dominated. Yasuko, the youngest of three daughters, had been adopted back into the Yokota family, although she was born Iwasa. She had been widowed twice and remarried a third time, each of her husbands adopting the Yokota family name, since there were no males in the family to carry on the name. Aunt Yasuko had five children now, but her third husband was drafted into the military along with most other eligible Japanese men.

In Sacramento, I quickly adjusted to American life. To keep up with *Nisei* friends, I learned English, competed successfully in school sports and got good grades, but still had to face the strict discipline of a Japanese classical dance mistress. I also had to do all the housework, since my mother was busy with her husband's liquor wholesale and retail business. Mother did not allow me to date, although I was chosen Miss Nisei Sacramento, representing the whole area's Japanese-American community at the San Francisco World's Fair in 1940.

My high school days were almost over when, to the shock of Japanese-Americans, Japan attacked Pearl Harbor. I never got the chance to finish high school.

Although historians argue over whether the United States received advance warning about Japan's Pearl Harbor attack on December 7, 1941, the infamous event provoked the virulent response of the nation's leaders and its news media.

At first, the F.B.I. picked up Issei leaders — Buddhist ministers, Japanese language teachers, newspaper editors and judo instructors — in unannounced predawn sweeps.

President Roosevelt signed Executive Order 9066 in February, 1942, authorizing the Secretary of War to designate military areas on the West Coast from which any or all (Japanese-American) persons could be excluded. For the hardworking Japanese immigrants and their American-born offspring, this meant the loss of carefully nurtured fields, simple homes, businesses, and constitutional rights as they were physically removed from their communities and herded into relocation camps. They suffered fear and anxiety over the safety of their families and their future well-being. Almost 120,000 people, most of them U.S. citizens, endured first the temporary assembly centers, then the concentration camps set up by the War Relocation Authority. These ten camps were scattered over the most barren and climatically severe spots in America. During their internment the Japanese were denied all due process of law. Some even showed loyalty to America by volunteering to serve in the U.S. military while their families were locked up in camp behind barbed wire.

We were packed off under guard to the Tule Lake concentration camp, in a bleak, mountainous part of Northern California near the Oregon border. The camp had the most pro-Japanese *Issei* as well as many *Kibei*, and it was known for its fights and other disturbances. Some internees repatriated to Japan during the war. Some just sat and waited for Japan to win the war.

I tried to finish high school in camp, but the American school was terrible — no one wanted to go there. The Japanese school in camp, which taught Japanese language and sponsored many cultural events, did well, under the circumstances.

As we were not allowed at first to have newspapers or radio news or entertainment from the outside world, occasional amateur talent shows provided a break from the dreary conditions of camp. I performed Japanese classical dance many times on the makeshift mess hall stage.

My family had "better" quarters in camp. My mother, who was very fussy, insisted we cook our own simple meals over the coal stove in our corner of the barracks instead of eating C-rations in the noisy mess hall. Camp was no picnic. Soap, fresh food and privacy were almost nonexistent but my mother continued to be proud and particular.

In camp I met George Tsutakawa, another *Kibei Nisei*, who was visiting his relatives while on leave from duty in the U.S. Army, where he taught Japanese language in the intelligence schools. His relatives and my parents arranged our marriage after we had met only twice (chaperoned visits at that!). We continued to correspond while I was in camp, but he was still a stranger to me on our wedding day.

In Japan, the other branch of the divided family lived out the war days with Aunt Yasuko, a rather shy, patient woman with a surprising sense of humor. Aunt Yasuko inherited the position of head of the family. One after another, weary and ill from the effects of the war, those around her died: Great-grandmother Take; then Grandmother Tsuta; then Yasuko's third husband, who had fought in the South Seas and returned to Japan only to be killed in a food riot; her older sister Masano; and finally, my favorite brother Takeo, who had become an army lieutenant. Takeo died while on leave in Hiroshima, in the world's first atomic bomb blast.

Yasuko buried and said prayers for them all. Soon after, she married the illiterate carpenter brother of her late husband — a fine man who adopted the Yokota name and raised her five children. The couple still lives in the Okayama farmhouse.

An incalculable number of people died in conflicts peripherally and directly related to World War II. Certainly, Japan's militarist actions took many lives in Asia, and in turn, many Japanese (and American) soldiers were killed. We can add to that the large number of the Japanese-Americans who died in the distant, isolated relocation camps, unable to procure adequate medical care from a hostile U.S. War Relo-

cation Authority.

But the final devastation came at the hands of the arrogant American government that wanted to prove to the world its superiority in technology and military strength. On August 6 and 9, 1945, the United States dropped atomic bombs on a country that had already lost the war, was dangerously low on food supplies and whose transportation lines were cut — a Japan whose spirit was gone and whose emperor planned to surrender within a few days.

Perhaps 250,000 persons, a large percentage of them elderly, many of them women and children, died in the atomic blasts. Offspring of the bomb victims continued to suffer from radiation illnesses, although the United States government denied that its little experiment on human lives caused such effects.

Japanese-Americans returned to the West Coast after the war to find their homes sold or abandoned by so-called caretakers, the contents scattered. At first many families huddled in church gymnasiums for lack of shelter. They faced long legal battles to reclaim their confiscated property and businesses, and most never were able to gain a satisfactory compensation for their losses.

My family was one of the first to leave Tule Lake, anxious to return and reclaim what we could of our businesses in Sacramento. I was sad and angry over the losses of the war, in particular the atomic bomb dropped by the American government which killed my dear brother. I delayed my marriage to George a year and a half, during which time I single-handedly managed the Iris Grill (named after me, since my name, Ayame, means Iris), a cafe in downtown Sacramento. Ironically, *Nisei* soldiers who had fought in the U.S. Army and were on their way home to Hawaii were some of my best customers. I guess I had learned some of the ways of my mother Kumano and managed the small restaurant just fine.

In 1947, when I was twenty-three, I moved to Seattle to marry George, an aspiring artist who worked in his relative's grocery store. I soon had four children — a son, a daughter, then two more boys. However, I knew few people in Seattle except my husband's relatives. George eventually finished graduate school and began to teach art at the University of Washington. Although I had secret ambitions of following my mother's footsteps in business, my children and my husband's work came first.

My mother continued to expand her shops in Sacramento to include a jewelry store. After her third husband died, she quit the other stores and opened a Japanese restaurant with her son Glen. Again, she worked day and night, not thinking about her family's history of problems with high blood pressure. She died from a stroke at the age of sixty-two. My mother had lived a fairly unusual life, far different from the stereotypical sheltered life people usually think middle-class Asian women enjoy. She had traveled, worked and seen businesses come and go.

Now I sit and reflect on the strength of those Japanese women in the early days and how they worked hard to keep the family going. I only hope the future generations remember and do the same.

The women in my family have supported the weight of centuries of feudal patriarchal practice, in which women did as much physical work as their male counterparts but got no recognition for their special role in keeping families together, and for passing on the cultural values. They suffered the tragic effects of wars as well as economic hardships and racial discrimination.

As the third- and fourth-generations of Japanese-Americans grow up in an ethnically diverse and fast paced society, it is not difficult to lose track of the histories of our families.

However, along with the kimonos in the pawlonia wood chest, we inherit the responsibility to know the fascinating stories of the women in our families. They are as brilliant or somber as the hues of these many kimonos, but the meaning of their lives, and the hardships they endured, will never fade.

J. T. Stewart

"Reports of Her Life Have Not Been Adequately Exaggerated": An Interview with Colleen J. McElroy

JT: *How would you introduce yourself to the readers of Gathering Ground?*

C: Well, primarily as a poet and as a poet who deals with people more than things, although I like to write about things. But my poems definitely have an American quality because I'm telling about what I am, usually about femaleness and Blackness and Black perspectives. I hesitate when someone says, "Will you identify yourself as a Black female poet?" as though I were a Martian. I see myself as I am which I use to define myself to myself . . . defining the world, then me: first to me, then to others.

When and how did you start writing?

I was introduced to poetry because I was married to a poet. I suppose that I've always done something in preparation for writing because I've been a storyteller all my life. As a child I gathered friends by having the ability, the facility for telling stories, for entertaining the neighborhood with one or another of the stories I would make up when I was by myself . . . and so poetry became a natural outlet for that. It became a way of telling those stories I had been telling about my family. I began writing officially, professionally, in my mid-thirties. And in some respect that was fortunate because I had written or I had gone through the stage of relying on cliches, of looking at easy situations. I had reached the point where I understood life to be complex, disappointing, and surprising.

Can you say how your background plays a part in your writing?

My father was in the service, so I spent a great deal of time travelling. We never stayed in one place for longer than three or four years. And so I learned to observe and make judgments very quickly because when you're the new kid on the block, the new kid in school, you can't afford to make too many mistakes unless you want to be totally outside. I've never felt that I've wanted to be an insider, but I didn't want to be totally outside. I had to make use of all that travelling I'd done. I learned how to cull from all my experience to interest the new kids . . . new to me. In that way, I suppose, I learned to observe. The other part was that because I didn't spend a lot of time in one place, I spent a lot of time alone. I was an only child for twelve years, and I had to entertain myself. And I did that by telling stories to myself. I would re-enact scenes or imagine scenes where I was anyplace but where I was. Because I could imagine myself where I wanted to be, the endings could be as happy or unhappy as I wanted to make them. Those are two things which are absolutely necessary in becoming a writer: observation, imagination.

Tell us about your recent promotion at the University of Washington.

Difficult is the way of describing it. It was not something I had prepared myself for; I had not said, "This year I am going to try for full Professor." By circumstance, situations worked themselves into a way that I could opt for a promotion or go somewhere else. What I discovered and what is probably true for most writers is that home is not the first place where you are recognized. So I found myself being recognized more and more as a writer and a teacher of writing in places other than Seattle and the University of Washington. And I found it more and more difficult to reconcile not being recognized for my talent, for the things I had achieved. At one point I felt that the reluctance to recognize me had to do with my being Black. But I eventually concluded that it had more to do with being female than it had to do with being Black in this case. You cannot separate being female and Black from the person that you are, so all of this is very arbitrary. I was very pleased to get the promotion, but I was surprised to find that the conflict over whether to stay or go somewhere else in a position of higher rank took more energy than I was in the position to give.

What are the personal and professional implications of being a full professor, as well as a Black woman, as well as a nationally recognized writer?

The personal implications are that I have to redefine myself constantly. You reach a point in your life that becomes an age of achievement; somehow forty is that magical point. It's really arbitrary, about as arbitrary as a twenty-four hour day, but when you reach that point you feel you have defined yourself in a certain way. And now I have to redefine myself; I have to redefine what my goals are going to be. It's not that I have to work for the promotion; the promotion has been achieved. Personally it means that I have more responsibility for other women on the faculty. Not to show them the way, that's ridiculous, but to show them what the process might be to achieve recognition.

My writing has never been to get the promotion. The writing has been something I do. If I don't write, I don't feel that I've managed my time, my personality . . . writing and the personality are so closely linked . . . so that I have done as much with that as I can possibly do. Writing will always be the primary thing I do, what I achieve; it will always give me satisfaction. It goes back to learning to live with myself. One of the things about the promotion is that it's like moving from one tax bracket to another. Now that I'm here, what? Well, I have to learn to live with myself. It doesn't give me any more years of life; my mortality rate is the same as it was before. I do this, the writing, because I have to do it, not because I was ordered to do it.

I have the distinction of being the first Black woman to become a full Professor at the University of Washington; that distinction doesn't necessarily mean a lot. On the one hand, it's something I did, and it's possible for other women to do. I don't want to be a spokesperson for a group, but I feel it is necessary for someone to say that the University of Washington has been there for a long time, and I am pleased to be the first Black woman Professor. Yet I think the honor is dubious because it has taken so long. And I think for me, personally, becoming the first does not mean headlines; it simply means this thing you have been working to do, you must continue working to do. I got there by being a writer. It doesn't mean I'm going to put down my pen. And I hope I will be viewed as the same kind of teacher as I was before I got the promotion, that the students will view me as an effective teacher — not because I got the promotion, but in addition to my having gotten the promotion.

Which of your own poems, stories, books have given you the most personal satisfaction?

The last one! It's always been my last one! When I got my first five poems published, the first time I sent out a batch of poems and got them accepted, even then it was my last one. I find that has not changed. Sometimes a reading (performance) may be a testing ground. When I feel that I have finished the writing, I stand up to read the work and as I'm reading I say, "This is NOT it! This does NOT work!" And so that piece changes from being my last one to my next to last one. Whatever it is that works, whatever it is that I feel pleased about is the one that gives me personal satisfaction. I can look at it and say, "Yes, I REMEMBER doing that!" For me one of the drawbacks of writing is the short term memory process. It's sort of like the birth process because if you remembered all of it, I'm not sure you'd go back so many times. I don't remember everything that goes into a piece of writing. I remember the general outline, the general step of one thing to the next. I can look at the intricacies, I can look at the subtleties and I know those things have arrived unconsciously somehow, or they have arrived without my consciously manipulating language. And for me that's the moment of the writer as effective as opposed to the writer as mechanic. There has to be some magic; it's reaching that point of magic that gives me satisfaction.

How do you feel about poetry and fiction? Do you prefer one form over the other?

I get more satisfaction out of having written a poem, a poem that I found difficult to start: not knowing where it was going, and feeling wonderful when I found out where it should go. With fiction I find that it drains me more. I'm more befuddled, I'm more un-settled when I finish it although it may be more worth the effort than the poem I've just done. My writing becomes more and more complex as I write. It's less reminiscent of the time when I used to sit down and tell the story of one of my uncles. It now, I think, reflects layers of meaning, layers of experiences. So I write less but when I write my writing is more involved. It reflects different areas of my life.

This summer, for example, I wrote two short stories and four poems, so I guess you'd say two poems for every story. But those stories didn't give me the same feeling as with the poems. The poems gave me a feeling of euphoria. With the stories I kept feel-ing, did I do that right?—should I go back to page nine? With the poem I carry the whole thing around in my head. With the story I carry it around in pieces. Someone else reading the story sees it as a unit; when I read it, I see it in various pieces. With the poem I see it in one fell swoop with its own movement, its own rhythm, what-ever. And that gives me a great deal of satisfaction.

What changes do you observe in yourself as a writer . . . let's say over the last few years?

It would be too easy to say that I'm older. I'm less satisfied with the easy way of finishing a piece. I'm more willing to try another version of it. I'm pickier, I don't know how else to put it; I'm harder to please. And it might be because I've read so much more. I've tried so many versions of how to write this thing down called "My Life," or "My Life as I See It." Also I am much less apologetic for being who I am. I believe I've always been independent. I also know that I am dependent, that I can be indecisive as well as I can be stubborn. Now I'm less apologetic about those shifts in my point of view. We used to call them shifts in mood, but this hasn't anything to do with hysteria or 'woman fever.' Certainly my shifts in point of view I recognize as being that's the way life is; and, I think without falling into cliche, I am much more aware of bonding—and particularly bonding between women. And I'm adamant on the notion that the older woman has more to offer than anyone on the scene has. I suppose there are people who would say, "You can say that because you're getting to be the older woman!" Certainly as a younger woman I thought I knew everything. As an older woman I know I don't know very much at all, but I'm trying my best to learn. It's never too late to begin.

As a writer what would you most like to do or accomplish?

I would like to have a body of work that reflects perspectives, and I can say this is the way I was when I was at this age or at that age. I want to keep writing. I will possibly write screen plays, things other than short fiction and poetry. Whatever it is, I want to keep writing.

Do you recommend writing programs/writing degrees for women writers, for women writers of color?

I think a writing program does one thing very well. It forces you to read a lot of writers in a very short period of time, whereas it may take you a longer period of time to stumble on the same writers. But I think any woman must choose a writing program with a great deal of care, and a woman of color must choose a writing program with a great deal of cynicism because these programs are generally not designed for achieving a goal as a writer but achieving a goal as a student. And it's far too easy for a woman to remain a student. You have to do something else to become a writer. But a writing program does immerse you in work, in writing by professional writers. Even then you must seek out those writers who will not be included in that course. You have to look at the bibliography in the back of the book. You have to go to the libraries and bookstores and browse.

There's no failsafe device that says any writing program will give you what you need to become a writer because when you're in the writing program, you don't really know what you need to become a writer. And neither will the instructors; they will merely give you some sense of technique. And from that sense of technique, you can collect those skills which will most benefit your writing. Still the skill you choose today may not be the one you most need in the future. The writing program is not the end of one's career as a beginning writer, as a student writer. You are constantly re-evaluating; I find that writers I could not abide five years ago are beginning to make sense to me now. Maybe it's because I've seen so much that I'm learning to deal with them now. Moreover, I was impatient and I would not deal with them; I wanted to move on to something else very quickly.

I've never gone to a writing program; I've never attended a writing class. I've taught them rather than been a student in one. But in the process of teaching them, I had to find out "Whom do you teach?" and "What do you teach them?" and "How do you say it?" For a woman of color, a writing program allows you to see where other writers are going. Hopefully, it allows you to see where the MEN are going! But it certainly allows you to see where the writers are going. And you can make some judgments about whether or not you want to go there. Whether you decide to go into a program or you don't, I say to students, "Read a writer even if it's only to decide you will NEVER do that!" But that's what a writing program does; it teaches you to read for the knowledge and skills. It doesn't teach you to be a writer. The writing you have to do.

Tell me, how do you define craft? What is most essential for a beginning writer to have?

An awe of language. A beginning writer must know that language is something with which you draw pictures with words. And language is like taffy; it can be pulled into shapes you can recognize. People always say, "Oh, I've written poems." But you must do more than those people do. You must use language to make your poem special. The language of poetry is a special tool; it's not the tool you use on the telephone to order a pizza. It's the tool you use to shape the world from which pizzas are made.

When I talked to you about how I got into writing, I stopped too short of the point. I got into writing, I think, because I've always loved language. Language has always been there, even when I didn't have words, I liked the way it sounded. I like the way foreign languages sound. I would like the way Martian languages sound. Nothing can draw me into a room quicker than the sound of language; it's something that's so fascinating, so magical. Words come out of somebody's mouth and something happens to the brain. I guess I could be a doctor of language. I look at language and I examine it, and I say, "Oh, God, look at what's just happened!" in the same way that someone does with a painting or with a dancer.

O.K., let's talk about Gathering Ground. In the initial flyer for this book, we (the editors) asked for writing that deals with three things: self-discovery, community perspectives, cultural awareness. Yet many of the manuscripts that we got didn't have anything to do with these themes. In fact, a number of women thought we were being vague or unclear. These responses puzzled us. Can you comment on this situation?

It's not vague to me. I think the thing about community might be difficult, at least for me because I think of myself as being in a community of women, but not every woman speaks the same language nor are all those women from the same ethnic background. The community that I'm thinking of does not have any geographic boundary; that's what I'm saying. Can I talk about a particular poem?

Certainly.

In "Caution: This Woman Brakes for Memories" (p. 175), it is that part of self-discovery — it's not just that humorous side of it — it's the use of graffiti because I'm an idiot for graffiti. I love graffiti because it says someone stopped and had a comment to make. But it also asks, how did I get to be this way? The discovery is constant and ongoing from one day the next. Most days confirm the last 300, but some days confirm the last little facet of it. But it's the process itself that counts.

You just anticipated something I was going to ask. You certainly don't shy away from these issues. In "Caution: This Woman Brakes for Memories," you deal head on with self-discovery. In "Upon Viewing a Photograph in Which I Stand in Shadow behind My Grandmother," you deal with cultural awareness and community perspective. Are these matters imperatives for you?

Oh, yes, definitely, and in that second poem more than in Caution:. . . " I'm notorious for going home and stealing photos. I steal photos of the family constantly. My mother will call me and say, "Do you have a photograph of . . . ?" And I say, "Who me? No, I never heard of it." Well, my mother's finally given in, and she's started sending me batches of photographs. I've put them away, and I've taken them out again and put them away. With this photograph of my grandmother, I'd looked at it a number of times and seen there was this figure standing back there. But one time I realized it was ME! And I went through this absolute shock because the face that I saw was mine but not mine.

It's a thing that writers use constantly. You pass a window and you see a face, and you say, "Oh, that's me!" Well, this is what happens in the photograph. And I think when I'm writing, the piece that I'm working on may not be autobiographical, yet it reflects me somehow. Pieces of characters, little bits of personality are mine; they just come out in this character. The way the poem is shaped has something to do with the way I see things, the way I think I am seen. In that poem it is that sense of community. How do you reconstruct that picture? How do you reconstruct yourself? How do you reconstruct a piece of life? I have other poems that are historical. In order to be able to reconstruct, I have to have a sense of community. I can't do that without knowing who I am and where I am.

Perhaps we were assuming too much. We were hoping other women writers of color had these same imperatives.

I certainly see these imperatives in women I read. I see them in Paula Gunn Allen's work; I see them in Paule Marshall's work; I see them in Alice Walker's work. I don't think it is unusual; I think they are something that women writers think about. And I know we talk about it. We spend a lot of time talking about how much of us goes into our poems. A poem may not be directly about us; it may get to the point of going from reality to absurdity. If this is really YOU you're talking about, are you the clown in the box or are you the tree on the corner? What I do in "Upon Viewing a Photograph . . ." (p. 181) is talking about life from two points of view, of life from two different perspectives. I think women writers do look at writing as a process of self-discovery. RESPONSIBILITY. It is the responsibility of the writer to reconstruct a feasible slice of what life means. We have to keep this responsibility in mind.

This is a teaching question. How can we encourage women writers, women writers of color to improve their writing and to deal with these kinds of imperatives we've been talking about?

Those are two different questions?

Right.

O.K., maybe I should deal with the second one first, deal with the imperatives. Not one woman can say it for all women or for people like her. If you don't consider those imperatives as part of your writing, no one else will. You always consider what you are writing; you are writing for strangers, you are not writing for your family. When you write for your family, they become strangers; and you must, then, make your imperatives clear to those strangers. By making them clear, you can't take the easy way by turning them into a slogan, an ad or a military campaign. They have to reflect you, the you knowing certain writing skills.

You make those imperatives clear because, one—you recognize them, and two—you recognize the craft of writing. You know the components of what it takes to make a piece of writing work. There is a Black woman who's driving a stock car, a fast car on the track. She doesn't get into that car because she knows where the door is; she has to know something else about that car. That's what makes her good; that's what makes her a winner. But because language is something that is used by everyone, there is this notion I run across, particularly in students, that everyone can do it. IT'S

JUST SOME WORDS YOU SAY. But effective writing means that you know the components of language, the inside components — the skeleton, the viscera of that form or writing that you're using. That is how you make those imperatives clear. You use those skills: metaphor, how to indicate time, transitions, details — to get your point across, to make your image clear, to put your picture into focus, to make your words echo so that you finally SAY something.

How do you view Third World women writers now?

I think more critics are beginning to look at Third World Women Writers as a viable force, not as an oddity, not as an exotic model that sort of pops up now and again. Women are being asked more and more to conferences, and I think the conferences involve types of women of color and not just a couple of Black writers. And in that way we get to talk to each other. The communication is there in stronger ways than it was twenty years ago. In the sixties and seventies when people said "minority," they meant Black. And I think now, that's not what it means.

What question have you always wanted to be asked by an interviewer?

I can't think of anything.

In closing this interview, would it be ok to say to anyone who wishes to find you, that you . . .

> intend to retreat
> to a cottage on the nearest
> warm beach
> collect all manner of fetishes
> wear only long dresses
> and circular jewelry
> appear only on a full moon
> and speak in signs *

I think that is exactly what you should say! It is wonderful that you remembered it!

---

*From "Penultimate," by Colleen McElroy, in *Lie and Say You Love Me* (Circinatum Press, 1981). The title of this interview, "Reports of Her Life Have Not Been Adequately Exaggerated," is taken from the poem by the same name, also contained in *Lie and Say You Love Me*.

Colleen J. McElroy

Caution: This Woman Breaks for Memories

When the air is thin with frost
I blow rings of ice smoke
as I did when I was young
and imagined myself grown
and never answering to anyone.
From smoke rings to pots
that became helmets and tanks
I dreamed a world where
color had no name and eyes
were tears holding light.

Without knowing the contours
of earth any rock
can become mountain and puddles
vast oceans of many legged beasts.
None of this is new,
all children are urged
to wander behind the facade
of what is real before
they are pushed into the serious
matter of living where they lose
the surprise of believing.

We become adults with only a toehold
on fantasy like shapes in the corner
of the eye vanishing upon inspection.
I can turn a phrase or bend a letter
under until *o* becomes *e* or *3*
evolving to *8* and simpler numbers.
No easy *girl* into *gril* but *loan*
into *god* and *home* to *bog*.
One blink and a sign that says
Warning: Truck Makes Wide Turns
can be easily misread as Caution: This
Woman Breaks for Every Turn
and everything is possible.

Yesterday as I crossed the flag
stones of a posh hotel foyer
I saw a fat rat grey and sleek
claws clicking like bright new shoes
on the slick tiles as he turned
and I heard him yell to passing birds:
look at me look at me go in and out
of revolving doors go pitty pat
on my rat like feet go into fake
sunshine and champagne and home.
The silk calla lilies nodded yes
and I believed them.

Today on the beach logs became chairs
dead bears, boats with roots like stars and
I was a ship sailing back to the beginning

A Question of Vital Statistics

There is nothing much to say about my life except
I was born and raised in Ashtabula Ohio with
three brothers, one of whom is a twin.

—Response on an application.

When did you notice someone was missing
Children are always disappearing
Early and of their own free will
That one you thought attached
Through umbilical preference
Is wandering the earth footloose
And fancy free, as my mother would say
That one has never been given
To remembrances and won't fit nicely
Like a puzzle piece or flying wedge
She is mentioned only because
She connected men who would not
Have otherwise met
But the daily beauty of this life
Leaves her ugly
So she leaves you to dream her
For years

Many families have children like this
Ones that leave intentionally
Or those accidentally left
In bus stations, divorces, some other
Family's annual summer picnic
Even those you may have wished away
And though you never really tried
To forget such things
Nothing should've gone this far
You have lived in several sections
Of the country and travelled extensively
But her name is lost except for the most
Tedious details

Now you try to assuage your guilt
Perhaps you once passed her without knowing
Perhaps despite your look-alike faces
You stared her down in some town whose name
Sounds like Ashtabula
Maybe it was her you saw under the fluted
Sky of marketplace umbrellas
Near Adana, Athabasca or Ashkhabad
Her smile vague behind the clumps of vanilla
Orchids and bayberry stippling the air
She was looking for what would bring her back
So she paid only for those things
That seemed strange yet familiar
Like toad water and square eggs
An image of one brother
Carved on her face forever

You try thinking of her as belonging
To those wonderful pictures of grey
Toothed women in the photo sections
On sunday supplements
You love the zen of it all
You are thinking of odd sizes
Timeless clocks and gimcracks
That will make her reappear
But even in Ohio you can only recall
The faint sound of her voice
Trapped like a pearl inside family myth
You are unaware that she has taken
To specially honed knives
That burn scars into the skin
Like paper cuts
It will be months before you realize
You've lost two maybe three fingers
On your ringless left hand and years
Before they're really missed

What Goes Around Comes Around and Goes

evenings yeasty with gossip
and sarcastic stories about what child
was gutsy enough to buck 1942 and the draft or
who still can't forgive Uncle Cohee's boy
grown stubborn and leaving his mama
for street-side preachers before
the rest of us had heard of Malcolm X—
grown stupid his daddy sneers forgetting
zoot suits/Father Devine/bootleg jazz
him robust—full of freedom's smell then and now
talk quiets down remembering the difference—
veterans lost in Harlem Race Riots
two aunts *passing* into another family's albums
those yesterdays grown old—fashioned when
folks insisted on coming back proud to color—
settling accounts of us against the world

supper visits nested in memories
talking despite teenage cousins snickering—
youth boasting independence with jewelry
on wrists/ears/nose and age outrageous with
hair-cuts/get-down styles smacking of anger/power
eyes crusty with how much this world ain't changed—
saying desist and adjust ain't in their vocabulary
what educates us to money is in no Book
and best don't mean last as they head for the door—
familiar beasts like in the sixties when we
would bust heads for less but now
Maddie averts her eyes cries lord chile
them fights were all for the chillun—
kids burst out laughing and family whispers cause
nobody respects truth more than its victims

At 102, Romance Comes Once a Year

(for Joseph Johnson, Seattle)

down in Banyantown where young
girls prance swaybacked
for strangers we hear tell
some folks be remembering how
old men used to work till
they nothing more than corn
cobs of brown skin waiting
for the holiday sun
to warm them red

upriver houses don't need much
care so the old men sit
by the shore where eddies
of water churn the air fresh
and they can mulch over
annual events and how too
many young girls go
bad all the time now

when hours paint houses sunset
orange old men who still be trying
to learn what the word *retire*
means to somebody who ain't never
been laid off try forgetting
their strokes and force angry
limbs to stiffly water lawns
while their gummy eyes
watch some woman's skirt sway

no matter where I go, Joseph
they all remind me of you
with your shoeshine stand and 100
birthdays but still not looking
a day over 65 by any real
calendar and as pretty black
as any woman be wanting
nodding yes when I whisper
magic names of lost cities:
Montego, Toberua, Titicaca, Tiv
Tupelo, Topeka, Tacoma

Upon Viewing a Photograph in Which I Stand in Shadow Behind My Grandmother

my arm bent as if waiting for a purse
or a cup of coins I am already turning
away from the cinnamon yellow woman
who spawned my mother and the rest
she is sitting at the edge of the lawn
her chair placed as if waiting for some
one who has been lost and the dog
her eyes those last years, seems the only
figure tilted in her direction

it is august, I'm sure, because the old
men have come out to water their lawns
and lean cane heavy into the afternoon
their limbs thick from strokes and eyes
milky pink inside faces washed in resent
ment of having been pullman car-porters
doormen-janitors and husbands of women
who have more power than the law allows
it must be dusk because my face is blurred

soft black in light still full of green air
and the window is unshaded where my uncle
who owns the house with his G.I. Pension
and sharp nosed scent of my intrusion has
already rolled back the blinds so neighbors
marked with the ease of color from soft
peach to licorice, can view the perfectly
placed lamp and prized wine decanter
these are our treasures and I am the figure
neither in the photo nor out of it

all movement is askew and on the verge
of tilting inward like my face that floats
in its own 15 yr old deliberation, eyeing
sideways the woman who signals her mortality
in the netting of lines feathered
beneath the fringe of fuzzy hair
where she smiles as if she knows
without turning that I am moving
in some other direction

Contributors' Notes

Cecilia Concepción Alvarez was born in National City, California, in 1950 to a Cuban father and Mexican mother. She was educated at San Diego State University and has shown her art work in the Northwest, California and Baja California.

Julia A. Boyd is a Black Womanist (to borrow a term from Alice Walker), a title and class that Black Womyn acquire at birth, as opposed to feminist—a title that womyn choose to adopt, only after they've become acquaintanced with the reality of struggle and oppression related to daily survival. She is also a mother/student/worker/dancer/reader of books that serve to enhance and broaden her awareness about Womyn of Color.

Sue Chin currently works as an editor at Metro, a public transportation and water quality agency in Seattle. She is a former editor and writer with the *International Examiner,* a community newspaper which covers the news of the Seattle International District and Asian American communities. She is active in local community affairs.

Jo Cochran, b. 1958 in Seattle, Washington. She is of Lakota/Anglo descent. She names herself an Indian Lesbian Feminist. Presently, she is finishing graduate work in Creative Writing at the University of Washington, where she co-instructs an introductory course in Women's Studies. She is also a coeditor for the special edition of *Calyx* on Native American, Chicana, Hispanic, and Latina women. In the other part of her life, she answers phones, sends out mailings, and does general office work for The Seattle Women's Gym. Mostly, she is interested in organizing the Old Feminists Academe and Retirement Home, and going there to live with her cat Bob-Robert.

Dorothy Cordova is Seattle-born and the mother of eight children. She is the director of the Demonstration Project for Asian-Americans, and a founder and member of Filipino Youth Activities.

Debra Cecille Earling: "I am a member of the Confederated Salish and Kootenai Tribes of the Flathead Reservation located in Montana. The story 'Perma Red' is based upon the life of my Aunt Louise, who died tragically in 1947 at the age of twenty-three. I am currently working on a novel about her life struggle. To the daughter of Louise, my sister Cheryl; and to the memory of my great-grandmother, Cecille Charlo Vanderburg, I dedicate this story. I am ever grateful to my mother, Florence McDougall Earling, for the gift of her stories."

Lisa Furomoto: "I was born in Honolulu, Hawaii, and am now a pharmacist at the University Hospital in Seattle. I am in love with a tall blonde and am crazy about the Northwest, but still miss visiting Grandma very much. Grandma is 86 this year."

Doris Harris — writer, poet, cartoonist and caterer — has lived in Seattle for nine years. The oldest of ten children, Doris was reared by her grandmother and the streets of Pittsburg. Doris states: "When writing this piece, I intended only a tribute to Black grandmothers. After raising my pen and wiping my tears, I witnessed 'Who Will Braid My Hair' emerge." Proud of her first published work, she's delighted it's about 'Grandmother' — her best friend and mentor.

Sharon Hashimoto's poems have appeared in *The Arts, Seattle Arts, Crab Creek Review, Poetry Seattle* and other journals. She has work forthcoming in the *Seattle Review.*

Kathleen Shaye Hill: "I'm an enrolled member of the Klamath Indian tribe; by blood quantum Klamath/Paiute/White. I have two (terrific) children, Shayleen and David Allen. I was scheduled to start law school this past fall, but the words of a former writing teacher, words once contented with merely nibbling at my brain, suddenly began voraciously gnawing. Her words? 'Sometimes you write a story because if you don't tell it, no one will.' That pretty well says it."

Edna Jackson, who lives in the small Alaskan native village of Kake, received her MFA from the University of Washington in Textile Design and has studied and exhibited her contemporary designs combining masks and weaving concepts in Washington and Oregon.

Nancy Lee Kennel, the daughter of a Japanese-educated Korean mother and an American father, grew up in Berea, Ohio. In 1977 she was a United States Presidential Scholar. After graduating from Yale where she majored in English and studied costume design, she taught English composition at Ewha Woman's University in Seoul, Korea. At present she is working on a novel as part of a research assistantship in Creative Writing at the University of Washington. She plans to become a costume designer.

Colleen McElroy has published five books of poetry, including *Lie and Say You Love Me* (Circinatum Press) and *Queen of the Ebony Isles* (Wesleyan University Press). She has been awarded an NEA fellowship, a Pushcart Prize, and Cincinnati Poetry Review first place poetry prize for 1983.

Amy Nikaitani, a Seattle native, was educated as a graphic artist and is largely self taught in charcoal and sumi ink drawing. She has exhibited in many local exhibitions.

Myrna Peña-Reyes was born and raised in the Philippines. She came to this country for graduate studies and earned a M.F.A. degree from the University of Oregon. She and her husband, William T. Sweet, live in Eugene, Oregon, where they own the Literary Lion Bookstore.

Kathleen Reyes grew up in Southern California and has lived in the Northwest for the past several years. Her poetry, articles and photographs have been published in various publications, including *The Portland Review, Clinton St. Quarterly,* and *Fedora.* She was a guest editor for the special Hispanic/Native American issue of *Calyx* (1984) and presently directs a poetry and fiction reading series in Portland called Glossolalia.

Vickie Sears is a Cherokee/Anglo living in Seattle, where she works as a writer, teacher and feminist therapist. Her poetry was recently published in the special Native American issue of *Sinister Wisdom, A Gathering of Spirit* (1983). Writing has been her dream since she was a child.

Charlotte Watson Sherman was born and educated in Seattle, Washington. While attending Franklin High School she was nominated for a National Council of Teachers of English Award in Writing. She has had poetry published in *Obsidian* and *The Black Scholar,* and gave her first public reading at a University of Washington Black Women Writers class. Charlotte is employed at the King County Jail and resides in South Seattle with her husband and daughter.

J.T. Stewart teaches at Seattle Central Community College where she directs the Writing Lab and is advisor for *The Ark,* the college literary magazine. She works with *Poetry Exchange* and is active in science fiction workshops and conventions. Some of her poetry and fiction appeared in *Nitty Gritty, Fog Cutter, Dark Waters, Backbone 2, Seattle Voice, Seattle Times, Star-Line Bumbershoot Performance Anthology, The Arts,* and *Nommo* (chap book). She is a trustee of the Washington State Commission for the Humanities. Ask her who she is and she will say, "I am a Black woman writer."

Bee Bee Tan, a Malaysian-born Chinese, has been published in *Focus* (Singapore), *The Seattle Review, Cargoes, Backbone II, 13th Moon* and other journals. She has given lectures and readings in Penang, Malaysia, Washington and Virginia, as well as special poetry workshops for children. Currently she is editing *Homegrown,* an Asian literary journal.

Barbara Thomas received her MFA from the University of Washington. A Northwest native, she has exhibited her art work both locally and nationally.

Essme Thompson has lived in the Northwest for ten years. She's worked in cable TV and computer repair, and is now concentrating on writing poetry, fiction and reviews of gay literature.

Mayumi Tsutakawa, a Seattle native who received her graduate degree in communications, is a former *Seattle Times* reporter and now a teacher at Seattle Central Community College. She previously edited the Asian-American cultural anthology, *Turning Shadows Into Light.*

Evelyn C. White is a Seattle journalist. She is currently writing *Chain Chain Change,* a handbook for Black women dealing with physical and emotional abuse, to be published by the Seal Press in fall of 1984.

Carletta Wilson has read poetry in galleries, schools, churches, coffeehouses and on radio. In addition, she has coordinated several poetry events, including Northern Lights and Neon Naturals: Seattle Black Women Writing. This is her first published work.

Yvonne Yarbro-Bejarano, a native Northwesterner, has been teaching Golden Age literature in the Romance Languages Department at the University of Washington since 1974. Her special interests include the literary work of Chicanas and political theater. Since 1977, she has co-edited *Metamorfosis,* a Northwest Chicano journal of art, literature and culture.